SELLING
FINANCIAL
SERVICES TO
Women

**What Every Man
Should Know and
Even Women Will Be
Surprised to Learn**

HOLLY BUCHANAN

HACHET PUBLISHING
Richmond, VA

Ordering Information

To order additional copies, contact your local bookstore or visit **www.SellingFinancialServicesToWomen.com**. Quantity discounts available.

Hachet Publishing Richmond, VA

Cover and Interior Design by Lightbourne, Inc.
Printed in Canada

ISBN: 978-0-9837765-0-5
Library of Congress Control Number: 2011916853

What readers of *Selling Financial Services to Women* are saying:

"If you are a financial advisor who is looking for a way to increase your business, look no further than Holly Buchanan's new book, *Selling Financial Services to Women*. Holly keeps you turning the pages at a quick clip as she combines valuable information with stories and specific tips on how to apply the knowledge to communicate more effectively with your clients whether they are women, men or couples. If you're not reading this book, you're going to be losing clients to financial advisors who are."

—STARR COCHRAN, CFP, EA, M. ED

"Successful financial professionals all excel at one thing, they know and understand their clientele. The very best producers (male or female) have fostered an exceptional working relationship with their female clients.

Understanding the differences between men and women, knowing communication styles, body language, risk tolerance and decision making processes set these financial professionals apart and drive their performance success. Are you missing these skills?

I have worked with Holly Buchanan and have learned a great deal from her, placing much of it into practice today. Enjoy her style — she is a pleasing read. Most importantly embrace and incorporate her essential action steps into your practice."

—RON SEILBACK, SVP, LTCI Solution Center Crump Life Insurance Services

"*Selling Financial Services to Women* by Holly Buchanan is a masterpiece on how to acquire and retain 'women' clients — one of the most under-served market segments across the world. If you are a financial advisor and serious about serving women as your primary target audience, this is your 'go to' book to discover and develop deep insights on women and finance. Holly's 'action plan to implement' at the end of every chapter on how to connect deeply with women clients is extremely engaging!"

—PARTHA IYENGAR, Founder and Managing Partner Accretus Solutions India LLP

"Finally a book that addresses the most important and growing market for advisors...female clients. Buchanan cracks the code for how to work most effectively with women. Whether you are a male or female financial advisor, if you want to grow your practice — read this book!"

— ELLEN ROGIN, CPA, CFP®, President, Strategic Financial Designs Inc., author of *Great with Money: The Women's Guide to Prosperity*

"Well, Holly Buchanan has done it again! Following the ground-breaking debut of *The Soccer Mom Myth,* that shared accurate and actionable insights in marketing to women, she has launched a new book: *Selling Financial Services to Women.*

Let me warn you in advance: This is not JUST about financial services. Oh sure, you'll learn why men see money as something that will grow and women view money as something that will be depleted. And, she shares rich, detailed insight into how to gain a woman's trust with broader, deeper conversations that help you understand her whole situation. And you'll learn the simple differences between how men and women view long term investments (Men want home runs. Women want singles.)

But this book offers so much more. You don't have to be a financial planner or CMO of a bank or insurance company to embrace the absolute gems she shares in this new effort.

Like just how important listening really is.

Why a man's status as a 'provider' is essential to understand.

The biological differences in male and female brains and what that means to each of them...and you.

Yes, this is a marketing to women book that anyone who hopes to increase their share of market with the segment that has the most influence, and buys the most, will want as their new roadmap to success."

— TOM JORDAN, Chairman and Chief Creative Officer HY Connect

To Suly Salazar-Layton,
For your big brain and even bigger heart.
De todo corazon, gracias.

CONTENTS

ACKNOWLEDGEMENTS

My biggest thank you goes to all the financial professionals I've worked with over the past several years. Thank you for sharing your stories, thank you for sharing your passion and thank you for the great work you do. I'm proud to know you.

Thanks to Suly Salazar-Layton for igniting my passion for the financial services industry. Thank you for expanding my mind, my Spanish vocabulary and my waistline from an obscene amount of sushi.

Mary Jane Fortin — Since our first meeting in Houston at the Mom 2.0 Summit, you have been an inspiration. Thanks for your superb leadership skills and setting the bar high for women in the financial field.

Special thanks to my research partners Stephen Reily at Vibrant Nation and Isabel Kallman at Alpha Mom. The insight from your audiences was priceless. Thanks for helping me shatter stereotypes about women and money.

Ron Seilback — You win the "guy who really gets it" award. Thanks for being such a vocal supporter and for writing the preface for the book. You rock.

To all the folks who read chapters and supplied invaluable advice: Kevin Riley, Laura Posey, Peter Walls, Tom Jordan, Lois Mellon and Amy Ewbank — this is a much better book because of your input.

For the experts who shared their wisdom — Margie Barrie, Annette Bau, Judy Hoberman, Jean Carpenter-Backus, Gerry Myers, Cella Quinn, Mary Moose, Amy McIlwain, Tony Fannin, TJ Couzens, Laura Posey, Alison Silbert, Wendy Boglioli and Shari Storm, you've made me and my readers smarter people.

And finally, to my family — Heather Buchanan for your spot-on editing skills, ability to laugh at the most inappropriate times and your homemade coconut cream cake...mmmmm, you're the best. And to Lee Buchanan, for being one of the first stewardesses to take to the skies, running your own business and caretaking a far from perfect family — you're one of the bravest women I know. Thanks for lighting the way.

PREFACE

Ron Seilback

If you're in the financial services industry, understanding women can be the key to your future success. Financial professionals who know how to attract, retain and communicate with their female clientele are going to have a competitive edge. As a financial advisor or insurance professional, women already are, or most likely will be your most important clients.

Regardless of their marital status — married, single or widowed — 95% of women are involved in household financial decisions and one-fourth act as the primary decision-makers.[1]

And as you already know, women outlive men. In the age group of 85+, there will be twice as many women living as men. That means women will eventually control the majority of Boomers' wealth.[2]

Today is the day to seize the opportunity to better understand, serve and sell to women. If you fail to act, you could be giving your competitors a head start in this important race. Your ability to maintain, grow and attract new clients is at stake.

I come from a brokerage general agency specializing in the Seniors Market, and I've worked with a lot of financial professionals. Successful financial professionals all excel at one thing, they know and understand their clientele. The very best producers (male or female) have fostered an exceptional working relationship with their female clients.

Understanding the differences between men and women, knowing communication styles, body language, risk tolerance and decision making processes set these financial professionals apart and drive their performance success. Are you missing these skills?

From personal experience, I have seen how a professional planner who understands women can grow his business and retain his female clients even upon the death of their spouse. (This is a critical time when many widows change advisors. Some reports say as many as 7 out of 10 women leave their advisors after widowing or divorcing.)[3]

My wife and I have a financial advisor, Tony Fusco MSFS, ChFC, CAP, located in Baltimore, MD. In our quarterly reviews he always maintains excellent eye contact with my wife, always seeks confirmation of understanding with her first and consistently recognizes her importance in the planning process. It's a win-win situation. I have certainly benefitted from his planning skills. And my wife appreciates and values the manner in which he seeks her opinion, confirms her understanding and demonstrates equal respect regardless of sex. Tony gets it.

Is he successful you ask? With a staff of ten supporting his organization and a client base nearing a thousand, what would you say?

You hold Holly Buchanan's latest publication in your hand. Will it drive you to a greater level of success? Only if you read the contents and apply the skills that Holly provides. Yes, I have worked with Holly Buchanan and have learned a great deal from her, placing much of it into practice today. Enjoy her style — she is a pleasing read. Most importantly embrace and incorporate her essential action steps into your practice.

Ron Seilback

SVP, LTCI Solution Center Crump
Life Insurance Services

INTRODUCTION

How This Book Can Help You
Grow Your Business

How you sell financial services to men is not the same as how you sell financial services to women. Men and women have different brains, different communication styles and different preferences and priorities when buying financial services and products. Even if they end up buying the same product, they may buy it for different reasons.

Some of the differences are subtle, which is why it's easy to miss them. And clients, especially women, are not likely to tell you about the things you do that turn them off. Almost every financial professional I talk to has a story of a meeting or presentation they thought went well, yet they didn't get the sale. I guarantee you many of these lost sales were due to a lack of connection with the woman, whether she was alone or part of couple.

Why does this matter? In a highly competitive marketplace, financial professionals who do a better job with women can easily win clients away from their competitors. (I've seen it happen). And, companies and professionals who do a great job of attracting new female customers bring in not only that one woman's business, but the business of her spouse, family and friends.

I've spent almost the last decade working with companies to increase their success in marketing and selling to women. The last several years I've focused on financial services because there is so much opportunity in this industry to reach out to female consumers. There is a huge amount of business to be won or lost.

A tale of two financial professionals

Financial professional #1

A couple of months after doing a seminar on connecting with women clients, I heard from an attendee. He was a financial advisor who had a client who was a widow. They'd worked together for several years. He knew she had some of her money with him, but knew there was more out there. He couldn't seem to get through to the widow to grow the account and play a bigger role in her financial planning.

After attending the seminar, he applied what he learned, including enhanced listening skills and relationship building techniques (which you'll learn in Chapter 6 — How to Sell to Women), with his female clients, including the aforementioned widow. An amazing thing happened. The widow transferred her entire portfolio to this advisor to the tune of, wait for it, 20 million dollars.

Financial professional #2

A couple with an extremely high net worth were being courted by some big-time money management firms. One firm picked up the husband and wife in a private jet and flew them to a fabulous location where they were wined and dined as company representatives made the pitch for the couple's business.

But in a conversation before the plane even took off, the financial professionals did something to alienate the wife. That's right, *before the plane even took off,* the deal was dead. Even though the husband might have been comfortable with the company, the wife was not, so their final answer was, "No."

That money management firm will probably never know why the couple decided not to go with them. But by failing to win the trust of the wife, they failed to win the account.

These scenarios play out every day. As I said, there is an enormous amount of business to be won and lost.

Huge opportunity

This is exciting news. There is an incredible amount of money either controlled directly or influenced by women that's up for grabs. A lot of your competitors are missing this opportunity. While many financial companies have woken up and realized that they need do a better job with women, very few have actually figured out *how.*

The companies, brands and individuals who do succeed with women are going to have an enormous competitive advantage moving forward. Women are earning more money, inheriting more money and participating more in financial decision making. And when you win the hearts and minds of women, you win the business of their male spouses as well.

Which brings up an important point. This book isn't just about selling to single women — it's also about selling to couples. One of the biggest mistakes some financial professionals make is focusing all their time and energy on the husband, not realizing the increasing amount of input and influence women have in the financial decision making process. Let them continue to disregard women. It only means more clients and money will flow to you.

NOTE: For all the guys out there asking, "Can men be successful in selling to women?" the answer is an emphatic, "Yes!" In polls, when asked who they prefer to work with, some women do indeed prefer to work with other women. Some women prefer to work with men. And most women want to work with whoever they connect with. So, there is an equal opportunity for all financial professionals to grow their business by doing a better job with women consumers. That's what this book is all about.

Here's what you'll learn:

1 — Why Focus on Women
Women are earning, inheriting and controlling more money than ever. Economic trends point to exponential growth in the economic power of women. And, hint, you especially need to focus on Boomer women. They're going to end up with all the money. *Seriously.* As an

added bonus, women are referral machines. Do a great job with her, and she'll recommend you to all her friends and family.

2 — What Do Women Want?

We'll unlock the mystery, at least as far as what women want from financial services professionals. We'll also look at what turns women off. Sometimes little things can cost you a sale. And women are very sensitive about being stereotyped. In this chapter I'll share some of the key insights from my Women and Finance Survey.

3 — Brain Differences Between Men and Women

We'll look at amazing brain research on the differences between men's and women's brains, how they are structured and how we use them. These differences affect how we perceive our world and make decisions, including how we make financial decisions. You will have many "aha" moments as you learn not only how we make financial decisions, but why.

4 — Male vs. Female Communication Style

It's been suggested that men and women are from different planets. Much of that has to do with our communication styles. Miscommunications and misunderstandings have torpedoed many a sale. Understanding the differences can help you be more persuasive and close more sales by speaking both languages.

5 — How Men and Women Look at Money

Men and women do not always look at money the same way. Their values, priorities, investment styles and timelines can vary widely. We'll look at those differences and how you can use them to create more persuasive sales pitches that hit the mark.

6 — How to Sell to Women

You'll learn specific techniques you can use to attract, sell to and retain female clients and customers. Building relationships and earning her trust sound like easy things to do, and they can be, if you know a few key secrets. Female clients who trust you actually use up less of your time and energy and remain loyal, even in market downturns. Yes, having a good track record is important, but not always the deciding factor for women. We'll look at what those deciding factors are and how to incorporate them into your prospecting and sales process.

7 — How to Sell to Couples

For many financial professionals, the majority of their business comes from working with couples. It's not always obvious which role each spouse plays in the decision making process. Even if the husband is leading the meeting and asking the majority of the questions, his wife may have veto power in the final decision. We'll look at how you can engage both spouses in important discussions and improve your sales process to meet both his needs and her needs. This is an especially important chapter for female financial professionals since we'll look at some of the common mistakes women make when selling to men.

8 — How to Sell Insurance to Women

Insurance is a women's issue. We'll look at why women are hardwired to want insurance and why they need insurance even more than men. We'll look specifically at how you sell life insurance, long-term care insurance and annuities.

9 — Referrals — How to Generate Word Of Mouth

Women refer more often than men. Women turn to other women in their trusted network for recommendations of service professionals (including financial professionals). Many financial successes are built on the power of referrals. Women can be referral machines if you know the right way, time and place to ask for and generate referrals.

10 — The Four Types of Female Customers

Not all women think alike. Once we've taken a high-level look at women, we'll zoom in and look at the four types of female customers you'll likely come into contact with. We'll give you specific tips on how to spot each type, questions to ask each type and sales techniques that match each investment style.

11 — Marketing Financial Services to Women

How do you develop marketing strategies and materials that attract women? We'll look at what images and language are most persuasive for women, and which marketing channels deliver the best results. You'll get specific recommendations in this chapter on websites, client events, trade shows, social media, email communications, Women's Advisory Boards and more!

12 — Women and Finance Survey Results

We'll go in-depth on the results from my Women and Finance Survey. I partnered with Vibrant Nation to survey women 50 plus (the ones who have all the money, and yet are often ignored). And I partnered with Alpha Mom to gain insights into women under 50 and moms in particular. The results surprised even me. You'll discover how women look at their finances and money, what their hopes and fears are and how they feel about financial institutions.

13 — The Client Meeting — Women-Winning Questions

What should happen in a client meeting with a woman or couple? What questions should you be asking your clients? The questions you ask are just as, if not *more* important, than the answers you provide. See a list of proven effective questions designed to gather key pieces of information and steer the conversation to the subjects women care about most. Follow these steps, ask these questions and close more sales. Period.

14 — Conclusion

We'll wrap it all up by reviewing the ways you can implement these techniques into your practice. Even small changes can have a big impact. I've worked with thousands of financial professionals (male and female) sharing this information on how to sell financial services to women. These techniques work.

What kind of results can you expect? If you make only one change to your business, you'll see an improvement. If you decide to make women a major focus, the opportunities are even greater.

For example, I recently spoke with a financial advisor who had seen my presentation a year earlier. He told me he took the information to heart and changed the way he did business, focusing on doing a tremendous job with women. A year later, he had doubled his business.

Banks, financial advisors, insurance companies and agents, investment firms — all can benefit. Success with women is the competitive advantage you've been looking for. Own that hill. Provide a superior experience. And watch your profits grow.

WHY FOCUS ON WOMEN

Many women are unhappy with financial services companies. A recent study shows 84% feel they are misunderstood by investment marketers.[1] The problem? Many women either feel current messaging and sales techniques are missing the mark, or that the industry is ignoring them completely.

Women are going in with low expectations. They're not overly delighted with the service they're getting, but they don't see anyone else out there who's doing a better job.

Here's why this is good news for you:

- No one owns the women's market
- Women have money and are a growing economic powerhouse
- Women are actively looking for financial guidance
- Women are referral machines

No one owns the women's market

Several years ago, a lot of financial institutions woke up and decided to focus more of their efforts on marketing and selling to women. But while many recognized the need, not all were successful in their efforts to connect with this market.

Some companies created a brochure or section of their website devoted to marketing to women. Some included a mom in the backdrop of their TV commercial. But that was as far as it went. Other companies and individuals have made more substantial efforts to market to women, but very few have succeeded in cornering this market.

Why haven't more companies been successful? Because it takes more than just lip service. It takes a consistent and company-wide effort to deliver a woman-friendly experience. But if you're willing to make that commitment, you'll get noticed. Because many women go in with low expectations, if you genuinely do a good job with women, they respond.

If you're looking for a way to differentiate yourself from your competition, focusing on women can be that differentiation point.

Women have money and are a growing economic powerhouse

Three factors are affecting women's economic power:
1. Women are earning more money than ever
2. Women are inheriting more money
3. Women are controlling more money by getting more involved in financial decision making

By now you've probably heard about "the rise of the wives" with almost one in four women out-earning their husbands. Boomer women are experiencing a double inheritance — inheriting from their parents and again from their husbands who they are outliving. And women are the majority of college graduates. All these trends point to the continued growth of women's economic power.

Not convinced? Here are a few stats:
* 57% of college graduates are women (U.S. Department of Education)[2]
* 22% of women earn more money than their husbands (Pew Research Center)[3]
* 89% of bank accounts are controlled by women (The American College)[4]

- 28% of homeowners are single women (Harvard Joint Center for Housing Studies)[5]
- Women hold 76 million credit cards compare to 68 million by men (Fast Company 2004)[6]
- As of 2009, Women controlled 33% of all private wealth in North America. That number is projected to grow at an annual rate of 8% worldwide through 2014. (Boston Consulting Group)[7]
- Between 2010 and 2015, an estimated $12.5 trillion will transfer into the hands of Boomer women. Most will eventually have sole custody of those assets, as they are likely to outlive their husbands (Council on Foundations and Community Foundations of America)[8]
- In 2009, 40% of private firms were at least 50% women-owned, compared with 26% in 1997 (U.S. Bureau of Labor Statistics)[9]

One note on women business owners — not only are they starting businesses, they are successful at those businesses. A few years ago I attended a Springboard Enterprises event at an investment bank in New York City. In case you haven't heard of Springboard Enterprises, here's the description from their website, www.SpringboardEnterprises.org:

"Venture-catalyst Springboard Enterprises is the premier platform where entrepreneurs, investors and industry experts meet to build great women-led businesses."

At this event, guys in fancy suits and ties stood up one after the other trying to court these highly successful women business owners. (It did my heart good.) These investment bankers were not there because it was the right thing to do. They were there because it was the *smart* thing to do. According to the Springboard website, 80% of Springboard companies are still in business, generating $4 billion in revenues and creating tens of thousands of new jobs.

In addition to earning and inheriting more money, women are controlling more money than ever. In more and more households, women are participating in the long-term financial planning.

Something financial professionals should be aware of is how couples shop for products and services. It is often the woman who does the initial research, gets recommendations and comes up with a list of possibilities. So you need to be on her radar screen in order to even be considered in the purchasing process. Yes, the husband may run the initial meeting, asking many of the questions. Some financial professionals take this to mean he is the one who is selecting the candidates and making the final decision. Men do participate in the final decisions, but there's a good chance it is his wife who is doing the initial research and influencing the list of candidates they choose from.

The other key point to remember is the fact that the wife is likely to outlive her husband. If you don't have a relationship with her, there is an excellent chance she will leave you for another advisor. Seven out of ten women leave their financial advisors within three years of widowing or divorcing.[10]

When I pointed this out during a seminar, a producer in the back of the room jumped up and ran out of the room. Later, during the break, he came up and apologized. He said his biggest client was seriously ill, and he realized he had no relationship whatsoever with the wife. He ran out of the seminar to call his clients and set up a lunch where he could start building that all important relationship with the wife.

Focus on women in your practice or in your company. The bottom line is that women are an economic force and key decision makers, and all indicators point to that trend continuing indefinitely.

Women are actively looking for financial guidance

When it comes to making financial decisions, a lot of men like to go it alone, take charge and be the master of their own domain. Men tend to rely more on their own judgment. Women are actively looking for guidance from financial professionals. They want someone to partner with to help them make smart decisions. Women are often more willing to ask for outside opinions. Even if she's still making the final decision, she is looking for guidance along the way.

This is excellent news for banks, financial advisors, insurance agents and investment professionals. She *wants* to do business with you.

Knowing this, I'm always surprised at the number of women who don't have a financial advisor or financial professional to help them with their financial planning. When I surveyed women about what's stopping them from getting the help they want, they cite two barriers:

1. They don't know a good advisor who they can trust.
2. They don't think they have enough money for a financial professional to be interested in working with them.

Let's start with the first point. Because so many women have not had a great experience, they don't have anyone they feel good about recommending. Women rely on recommendations from friends and other trusted sources. This is why financial professionals who DO connect with women enjoy so many referrals. When women have a good experience, they notice and WANT to spread the word. They trust that their friends and family are going to have a good experience with you, which is super important for women.

On the second point, I spoke with a widow who told me, "No financial advisor would want to work with me. I don't have enough money." It turned out she had almost two million dollars in assets. But some women feel these services are only for the uber rich. NOTE: All those grandiose commercials talking about "wealth management" only add to this perception. So if she tells you she doesn't have much money, do your homework. She may be more affluent than she appears.

So, women want to work with a trusted professional, but many have not found that person, meaning there's a lot of business out there to be won, and won easily if you know how to truly connect with women clients.

Women are referral machines

Because so many women are looking for financial guidance, and because so many have had bad experiences, when a woman has a good experience, she notices. And, an even more beautiful thing, she now has someone she feels good about recommending. Ask any woman where she found her financial advisor, insurance agent, CPA, lawyer, etc. and she'll likely say, "A friend recommended him/ her." Women trust other women when it comes to choosing a service professional. Do a terrific job with her and watch the power of word of mouth as new prospects walk in the door. We'll talk more about how to generate referrals in Chapter 9 — Referrals — How to Generate Word Of Mouth.

ACTION STEPS:

✳ Make focusing on women a company-wide priority. Don't just create a brochure or website. Look at the entire customer experience through the eyes of your female customers and find ways throughout to make it better for women. A great way to do this is to create a Women's Advisory Board which we'll look at in Chapter 11 — Marketing Financial Services to Women.

✳ Let women know you want to work with them and be a partner in their financial decision making. Reach out to women directly. (More on this in Chapter 11 — Marketing Financial Services to Women)

✳ Be the first in your area to focus on and own the women's market. Gain a competitive advantage and grow your bottom line by winning the hearts, minds and business of women consumers.

CONCLUSION:

Women are a growing economic powerhouse. They are actively looking for financial guidance. Focus on doing a great job with women and gain a valuable competitive advantage. The secret to success is to truly understand women and their needs. So what do women want? We could all make a lot of money with the answer to that question.

WHAT DO WOMEN WANT?

That is the question, isn't it? Let's start out with what women *don't* want.

Women don't want:

- To be stereotyped
- To be talked down to
- To be judged (put down for past mistakes)

Women do want:

- To be included and have their voice heard
- To be educated and to feel confident
- To discuss their individual situation — don't push "one size fits all" solutions
- To have a long-term relationship

In my previous book, *The Soccer Mom Myth, Today's Female Consumer: Who She Really Is, Why She Really Buys*, Michele Miller and I surveyed women from all over the country looking for soccer moms. There was just one problem, very few women self-identified as a soccer mom. They told us it is a stereotype, and a negative stereotype.

For example, take my friend Sally. Sally was a high powered executive, traveling the globe and working on high profile accounts. She took ten years off to have four kids. Sally was used to being addressed in a certain manner in her corporate years. But she was now seen as a stay-at-home "soccer mom." She said to me, "Holly, people talked to me like I was stupid." All they saw was a stay-at-home mom of four instead of an Ivy League-educated, hugely accomplished business woman.

Be careful of stereotyping. That "soccer mom" in your office is probably a highly educated, experienced and savvy woman.

Women want to be included

Don't make the mistake of talking down to women or assuming her husband makes all the big financial decisions. Even if you think you're doing a good job of talking to the woman, really pay attention. In my Women and Finance Survey I asked women:

**Who do financial advisors focus their attention on —
men or women?**

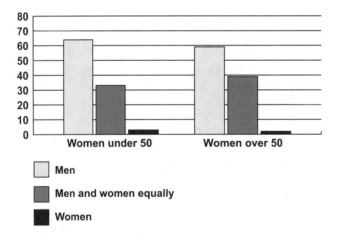

In your next meeting with a couple, focus on who you are talking to, who you are making eye contact with and to whom you are directing the majority of your questions.

Even if he is driving the conversation, make sure you are taking time to stop and ask the woman what she thinks and what her concerns are.

Women want to feel confident

Women are actively looking for financial information. In my Women and Finance Survey, women looking for financial advice turn to trusted sources like family and friends first, with the Internet a close second. They are turning to the Internet because they aren't getting that information from their financial advisors. Be that trusted source. Provide her with information. Want to win a woman's business? Educate her and increase her confidence.

Women want a long-term relationship

The other key way to win a woman's business is by building a relationship. Gather information about her whole life so you can make recommendations for her individual situation and needs. And communicate, communicate, communicate. One of women's biggest complaints is that they don't hear from their financial person often enough. I know your time with each client is limited, but remember, every touch point, every conversation is an opportunity to uncover new or changing needs which often lead to new sales opportunities.

We'll go more in-depth on all of these topics in Chapter 6 — How to Sell to Women.

How to Lose a Sale to a Woman

Scenario 1:

A couple comes into your office. The man is doing most of the talking, asking the questions. You address all his questions, lay out your track record and plan. You all shake hands at the end. The meeting went great. You're fully expecting the couple to do business with you. But they end up going with someone else. What happened?

Some couples have an understanding that when they are in public, the husband will take the lead. Even though the man is leading the conversation, the wife still has input into the decision. But you wouldn't know that from her lack of participation. The scene changes when they leave the office and get to their car. If the husband turns to his wife and asks, "So, what did you think?" and the wife answers, "I didn't like him," or "I don't trust her," Boom! You're dead in the water. Smart husbands know they don't want to make a decision their wife won't be happy with. You see, women have a super power, it's called "Veto Power," and it kills more sales than you know.

Smart professionals use this information to their advantage. I was talking with an advisor who told me this story, "A man came in and said he was looking for a new financial advisor. We had a great meeting. At the end, I asked if we could set up an appointment to bring in his wife so I could meet her as well. Well, a few weeks later, the guy came back and announced the couple had chosen me as their financial advisor. He told me, 'You were the only advisor who asked to speak to my wife.'"

I know there are some situations where, despite your best efforts, it's difficult to get the wife to engage in a meaningful way. There are specific questions you can ask that will draw her into the discussion. You'll find out what those questions are in Chapter 6 — How to Sell to Women and Chapter 13 — The Client Meeting — Women-Winning Questions.

Scenario 2:
You're meeting with a woman who has expressed an interest in a financial product. You've listened to her situation, explained the product and how it's the perfect fit for her needs. All her signals indicate she's ready to buy. So you move in for the close, but she won't commit. She says, "I need time to think about it." You end the meeting, thank her for coming in, and say to yourself, "Didn't make that sale. Time to move on to the next one."

Here's the thing, she was not necessarily saying, "No." When a woman says she needs more time to think about it, she is saying one of two things: "I really do need some more time to think over my options, do a little research and gain more confidence this is right for me," OR she is saying, "I have a concern/objection that's preventing me from feeling comfortable enough to say, 'Yes.'"

Women can sometimes take more time to make a decision. It is NOT that they aren't capable of making decisions. It is simply that they can have a more deliberate decision making process. They can also have more concerns and objections. We'll take a closer look at this when we talk about brain differences in Chapter 3 — Brain Differences Between Men and Women.

Before she leaves your office, set up your next meeting when you can hopefully close the sale once she's had time to process information, do more research, etc. Also, before she leaves, ask her one final question, "Are there any concerns I haven't addressed?" If she has an objection, wouldn't you rather get it out while she is in your office and you can address it?

It's important to close sales, but it's also important to give her time if she needs it. There's a fine line between being persuasive and being pushy. Cross the line into pushy and you'll destroy her trust.

ACTION STEPS:

✳ Assume both spouses are involved in the decision making. Focus your attention on her as well as him. Ask her what she thinks and what her concerns are.

✳ When discussing her financial situation, ask her about her financial successes as well as looking at the mistakes. Don't use judgmental language.

✳ Educate her about products and options.

✳ If a woman says she needs more time, she is not necessarily saying, "No." Set up another meeting and give her time to process the information you've shared.

✴ Communicate more often by email, phone, newsletters, greeting cards. The more you communicate, the more she feels valued. Build that relationship and identify new sales opportunities. You'll find specific recommendations on communication in Chapter 11 — Marketing Financial Services to Women.

CONCLUSION:

If you're a financial professional, take an honest look at how you work with your female clients. Look at your top couples. Do you have a relationship with the wife as well as the husband? Is she sending you referrals? If not, you may not be doing as good a job as you think. While men tend to be more direct, many of the signals women send can be subtle, so they are easy to miss. What are these differences and how can you spot them? Let's take a look.

BRAIN DIFFERENCES BETWEEN MEN AND WOMEN

A couple comes into your office. As you strategize about how they can save for their children's education, you notice a difference in the types of information they want from you.

The husband wants to know:

- What vehicles can they use to generate the best return on their money so there'll be enough money to put both kids through school?
- What are the numbers? How much does he need to save, where does he put that money and how much does that money need to grow between now and the time his kids are ready to go to college?

The wife wants to know:

- What happens if the stock market tanks?
- What if they need to tap into that money in case one of them loses their job?
- What if college tuition is way more expensive by the time her kids are grown?
- What guarantees come with the plan?
- What if one of their children decides not to go to college?
- Are there other saving vehicles they can look at to compare with the one you are recommending?

To many financial advisors, the wife's questions can seem like an attack. They wonder why she's pushing back so hard against their recommendation or trying to take the conversation off track.

Here's the thing, she's not attacking you or your recommendation. She's simply using a female decision making process. Her female brain wants more information, wants to plan ahead to avoid problems and wants guarantees of safety and security.

Her husband's decision process is based on numbers, goals and opportunities. He is using his male brain to focus on an end goal and a linear way to achieve that goal.

Many sales are lost because of misunderstandings about how men and women make buying decisions.

We all notice the difference between men and women in our personal lives. Men really don't like to ask for directions, and women really do remember exactly what you said in a fight two years ago. Men like to make quick decisions, "It's a tent, it holds four people, let's buy it." Women tend to want more information, "It's a tent, it holds four people, but is there enough room for all our packs and supplies as well? How hard is it to set up? Is it really waterproof? How durable is it — does it have double stitching? Why don't we go online and look at customer reviews."

It is not that one person's buying process is right and another's is wrong. It's simply different. In just a moment we'll give you insight into both his and her decision making process.

Many of those same differences at home are at work in professional and sales situations. While most people recognize certain patterns of behavior, they don't always understand the reasons for those behaviors. There's actually a wealth of scientific research, some of it fairly recent, that provides valuable insights into what men and women do, but also *why* they do it.

This science has made a huge difference to the success of my work and training. When I speak at conferences, attendees give my seminar high marks, commenting on how helpful it is to understand the science behind our differences. It's easier to understand *what* people want when you understand *why* they want it. There are many real "aha" moments.

So let's start with the science, and how our differences affect how we perceive the world, make decisions and communicate. These differences have a direct impact on how we make financial decisions and how we buy financial products.

Giant Disclaimer: Before we jump in, let me make one thing clear. There are proven differences between men and women. There is no suggestion that one is better than the other. Women and men both have wonderful natural skills. Also, not all men think alike, and not all women think alike. Some women reading this may have more of a male decision making style, while some men may relate more to a female decision making style. But there are some general differences that are important to understand. It can make a huge difference in how effective you are as a sales person.

Overview of Brain Differences

There is amazing new research on brain differences between men and women. Researchers put men and women in an MRI and see how different parts of their brains light up when they process information and make decisions.

In their book *Leadership and The Sexes, Using Gender Science to Create Success In Business,* Michael Gurian and Barbara Annis point out that neurobiologists have been able to track over one hundred biological differences between the male and female brain.[1]

These differences are important because how we use our brains affects how we experience the world, how we make decisions, what we buy and why we buy it, including financial services. In a selling situation, men and women may require different information, presented in a slightly different manner based on how their brains operate.

Here are some of the main brain differences. Again, these are generalities that won't apply to everyone, but it's helpful to understand the distinctions.

DECISION MAKING PROCESS		
	MEN	**WOMEN**
1	**Process quickly**	**Process completely**
	Brain differences	
A	Want to take action	Want to think it through
B	Compartmentalized thinking	Holistic thinking
C	Prioritize options	Compare options
2	**Focus on immediate gains**	**Focus on long-term benefits**
	Brain differences	
D	Short-term planning	Long-term planning
3	**Focus on achieving goals**	**Focus on achieving goals and avoiding bad outcomes**
	Brain differences	
E	Motivated by rewards	Motivated by consequences

#1 — Men process quickly — Women process completely

One of my favorite stories about the differences between men and women is the story of the rabbi and his wife.

The rabbi describes the way his wife tackles obstacles as full of drama: She rages, she cries, she internalizes everything. Her system of problem-solving takes a long time and involves making everything personal, leading with her emotions in a quest to see how she would feel about each possible solution. It is apparently a very stressful process. In contrast, the rabbi's problem-solving method is to just try to find the fastest fix. *Yet he prefers his wife's method.* When asked why, he said it was because, "Her decisions always end up being the right ones, whereas mine always end up being the quick ones."[2]

A common frustration I hear from sales people is that women can't make a decision. Let's clear this up. It's not that women can't make a decision; it's simply that women often have a more deliberate decision making process. Women tend to want more information before they make a decision. Many sales people I interview remark that women ask more questions in the sales process. Why is this?

Brain Difference A:

Men are hard-wired to take action — Women are hard-wired to think it through

Researchers have found differences in how men and women use their brains to react to different situations, especially in response to stress and anger. Men's externally focused brains in conjunction with testosterone often trigger an action response. Think "fight or flight." For women, their internally focused brains in combination with estrogen and oxytocin (a bonding hormone) trigger a "tend and befriend" response.

When men are stressed and face challenges, they want to take action. When women are stressed, they want to gather the wagons and talk it through.

Men's brains tend to focus on the gist of a situation. Women's brains tend to focus on details.

This is why everything matters in a sales pitch. She is looking not just at what you say, but what you're wearing, what's in your office and how you treat the waiter/waitress at lunch.

And just to clear up another mystery, scientists have noted that women encode memories with more emotional details. In *Brain Rules*, author John Medina points to research on this issue that states, "Women recall more emotional autobiographical events, more rapidly and with greater intensity, than men do."[3] This may explain why two years after a fight, women can remember everything that happened and exactly what was said, while men can barely remember what the fight was about.

Brain Difference B:

Men use compartmentalized thinking — Women use holistic thinking

Women have more connections between the right and left hemisphere of the brain. She's often pulling on both sides of her brain when she's making decisions.

Men tend to have more compartmentalized brains, often using one side of the brain or the other. They focus on one thing at a time and don't like to be distracted. Women tend to multi-task, moving from one task to another, often juggling several plates in the air at once.

With their efficient, focused brains, men want to narrow down their options until they find one solution that solves the immediate problem.

Women, with their more holistic brains, often pull in more criteria, expanding the search to find the solution that meets as many needs as possible.

Women also tend to have longer checklists of things that matter to them when making a buying decision, like choosing a financial advisor. That longer checklist of what matters leads to more questions and more research during the buying process.

Example: Choosing a financial advisor

Men:
- What are his/her credentials?
- What kind of a track record does he/she have?

- What's his/her investment strategy?
- What are his/her fees?

Women:

- What are his/her credentials?
- What kind of a track record does he/she have?
- What's his/her investment strategy?
- What are his/her fees?
- Does he/she work with people like me?
- What experience have others had working with this advisor?
- How much money do we need to invest with him/her in order to get truly personal attention?
- How much communication can I expect?
- What are his/her values?
- Can I trust this person?
- What if the person leaves their current company?
- What if this company goes out of business?
- Is this someone I feel safe with or will he/she be judgmental about our current situation?
- Will he/she use a lot of technical jargon or will they speak to me like a human being?

Women want many of the same things as men, they just want more. By meeting her longer checklist, you're also satisfying him as well. The extra information she gathers can help both of them feel more confident in the decision.

One other interesting note, all those extra connections between the hemispheres also help explain women's verbal abilities. Women use both hemispheres when speaking and processing verbal information. Men primarily use one. Women can more easily connect the right side of the brain, the home of emotion, with the left side of the brain, the home of speech. They can more easily express what's going on in their hearts and heads. We'll explore this more in Chapter 4 — Male vs. Female Communication Style.

Brain Difference C:

Men prioritize — Women compare

Men have more gray matter, women have more white matter. In human brains, gray matter represents information processing centers, whereas white matter works to network these processing centers.

He's designed to process quickly. She's designed to process completely. (Remember the story of the rabbi and his wife?) He's prioritizing — she's comparing all the options. She's trying to find the perfect solution for everyone involved.

For example: Gloria is planning the family vacation. Her husband just wants to go somewhere warm for a cheap price. He suggests an all inclusive resort in Cancun that he found online. The price was right and he was ready to book. But Gloria wanted to do more research. So now she's looking at accommodations, dining options, recreational activities, spa services, and "Oh, do they have reliable medical facilities nearby?" She visits review sites, talks to friends and has lunch with an acquaintance who's a travel agent. She now comes back to her husband with three choices, including his. He doesn't understand why they couldn't just book the place he found. Gloria thinks, "This is why I have to do the vacation planning. My husband simply doesn't think these things through."

Gloria is hard-wired to plan ahead and gather a lot of information before she makes a decision. Whereas, "good enough" works for her husband, Gloria wants "the best possible choice."

Women compare options when they're making financial planning decisions. If you make a recommendation for a solution, she may ask a lot of questions. Remember the opening scenario. All those questions were not an attack, but simply her way of gathering information and comparing options to find the best possible solution. Answer her questions, help her compare options and show her how this is the best possible solution for her situation.

For example, instead of saying, "You should buy an annuity," help her compare options. "You could put this money in a CD. Or you could buy an annuity. Here are the pros and cons of each choice." By all means recommend the option you feel is best. She wants your guidance. But she'll have more confidence in your recommendation when she's able to comparison shop and make sure it's the best possible solution.

ACTION STEPS:

✳ If you're delivering a report, have a report or chart that gives the executive summary and a thicker report with more details if she wants them.

✳ Be prepared for questions and understand they are not an attack, but simply her way of checking off items on her longer checklist.

✳ Give her time to process information then come back at a separate meeting to make a final decision. While he may want to narrow down options and take an immediate action, she may want to compare all her options and think it through.

#2 — Men want an immediate gain — Women want long-term benefits

My friend Michele was buying a big screen TV with her husband. He wanted to buy it so that weekend they could watch the game on the big new TV. She wanted to buy it so at Thanksgiving, many months in the future, when the family came over, instead of disappearing to the sports bar, everyone could stay home and watch the game on the big screen TV together.

Research on consumer purchases shows that men often focus on the near-term benefit, while women care about the long-term benefit. Joseph Carrabis, Founder and Chief Research Officer at NextStage Evolution, found in his research that, "Women purchase strategically; men purchase immediately."[4]

Brain Difference D:

Men focus on short-term planning — Women focus on long-term planning

There's an area at the front of the brain involved in long term planning including problem solving, emotion, judgment and complex thought. It also measures future consequences of current actions. (More on that next.) In *Brain Rules*, John Medina notes that, "Labs — headed by scientists of both sexes, I should perhaps point out — have found differences in the front and prefrontal cortex, areas of the brain that control much of our decision making ability. This cortex is fatter, in certain parts, in women than in men."[5]

In 2001, researchers from Harvard found that certain parts of the brain were differently sized in males and females, which may help balance out the overall size difference. The study found that parts of the frontal lobe responsible for problem solving and decision making and the area responsible for regulating emotions were larger in women.[6]

Researchers are still debating what these differences mean, but we know from evolution that men, the hunters, needed to focus on immediate needs, while women, the gatherers and caretakers, needed to plan ahead to make sure they had enough food for the winter and had everything necessary to care for children and family. Some of this ancient hard-wiring may still be at work.

Women are doing a lot of long-term planning and comparing many options to find the best one to meet their needs now and in the future. Men are excellent strategic thinkers and planners, but it may simply be that women value long-term benefits more than men do. In my Women and Finance Survey, we found that one of women's biggest financial fears is outliving their money (especially for women 50 plus). They're looking ahead and wondering what will happen if they live to be 90 or 100. They have no idea how they're going to plan for that.

#3 — Men are focused on achieving goals — Women are focused on achieving goals and avoiding bad outcomes.

Men focus on, "How do I get there?" Women focus on, "How do I get there, and what could go wrong along the way?"

How many times have you gotten in the car to go somewhere, and the wife or mother says, "Let's pack an umbrella, bottled water, an extra sandwich, a map, our emergency roadside kit.... just in case." *"Just in case,"* isn't something you often hear men say. Men focus on what's necessary (they are very efficient that way). Women focus on the "what if's?"

Mothers are experts when it comes to the "what if's?" For Christmas, my friend Mary Anne's mother gave her an emergency tool designed to break the windshield of your car should you become submerged in water. (It even had a blade to cut through your seatbelt. I kid you not.)

Women tend to focus more on risks. Note that I am not saying women are necessarily risk *averse*. They're more risk *aware*, focusing on safety and security.

In my Women and Finance Survey, we gave women a choice between reading two articles, "The four secrets to having the retirement of your dreams," or "The four biggest mistakes in retirement planning and how to avoid them." Here are the results:

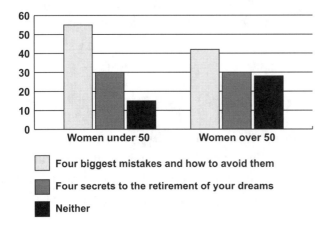

- Four biggest mistakes and how to avoid them
- Four secrets to the retirement of your dreams
- Neither

In both studies, the majority of women chose "The four biggest mistakes and how to avoid them." When it comes to financial planning, women don't want to make a mistake. They look at what might go wrong and want to make sure they are protected (right now many men are feeling the same way.) A lot of financial advertising is about achieving goals. I'm not saying that's a bad thing, but there are opportunities to create marketing materials that also address preventing bad outcomes. We'll explore this more in Chapter 11 — Marketing Financial Services to Women.

Brain Difference E:

Men have an active reward center — Women have an active consequence center

In a research study, men and women played an investment game while their brains were scanned by an MRI. In men, the reward center of the brain lit up as did the area that calculates numbers. In women, the reward center lit up, but so did the worry and error detection center. Women continued to think about the game and the *consequences*.[7]

This is important. Men were focused on rewards. Women were focused on the rewards but also the consequences.

Research in this area is ongoing, but studies show gender differences in the worry, anxiety and error detection areas of the brain. This could directly affect why women are more risk aware than men.

ACTION STEPS:

✳ Be sure to include the woman in any long-term planning or insurance discussions. She may be your biggest ally. Insurance can be a tough sell because most people think they won't see benefits for years or even decades (if they see benefits at all).

Men especially struggle with this. We'll talk more about that in Chapter 8 — How to Sell Insurance to Women.

✳ Ask women, "What are your concerns?" Remember women's preferences for articles focusing on mistakes and how to avoid them. He may be more focused on gain. She may be more focused on pain.

✳ When risk is involved, clearly explain the risk. The more information she has, the more trust she has in you, the more confidence she'll have in the decision or product she is investing in. Women will take on risk if they understand what the risk is and how it fits into their overall plan.

CONCLUSION:

More brain research is being conducted every day, and we continue to be amazed by what we're learning. The differences between men's and women's brains affect everything we do, including how we make financial decisions.

The best way I can sum up those differences is to quote Elizabeth Pace in her book *The X and Y of Buy: Sell More and Market Better By Knowing How the Sexes Shop:* "It's about his quest and her nest."[8]

Again, let me stress that there is no suggestion that one brain is better than the other. Men and women have many complimentary skills. Also, remember that these are generalities. Many women in the financial industry relate more to the traditional male decision making style. But understanding how our brains are wired and how that affects our decision making process can be an incredibly valuable tool when selling financial services.

4

MALE VS. FEMALE
COMMUNICATION STYLE

Meet Dean. Dean's wife needed to get up early the next morning to head out of town. Loving husband that Dean is, he offered to set the alarm and make sure his wife was up on time. Dean asked his wife, "What time do you need to get up?"

Dean's wife responded, "Hmmmm, well . . . I need to take a shower and leave a little time to figure out what I want to read and pack it into my carry-on bag. It takes about 45 minutes to get to the airport, but there shouldn't be much traffic that early in the morning. And I'm not sure if I'm going to have time to finish the report tonight, or if I'll have time to work on it on the plane. And do the kids have something for breakfast or should I make some oatmeal and leave it for them . . ."

As Dean told me this story, he admitted, "I just wanted a *number*. That was it. A number I could punch into the clock. Was that too much to ask for?"

Meet Sandra. Sandra is a life insurance agent. A couple has contacted her to talk about purchasing a life insurance policy. The couple only has one hour before they need to pick up their daughter at swim practice. Sandra is doing a needs assessment, but every time she asks a question, the wife seems to get off track.

Both spouses work. When Sandra asks the husband about his salary, he responds with a number, $120,000 a year. But when Sandra asks the wife about her salary, the wife goes off on a tangent:

"Well, there's the salary I'm making right now, but that could change soon. I don't know how long I'm going to stay at my job full time. We're thinking of having another child, and if that happened, I'm not sure if I'd take maternity leave or perhaps switch to another job or just stay home if we could afford it. But I've always been interested in starting my own business. How do you like being an insurance agent? Do you have much flexibility? It is hard to get started?"

Notice a difference in the answers? Have you run into similar situations?

Men and women have different communication patterns and styles. Linguistics researcher Deborah Tannen and biological anthropologist Helen Fisher have done extensive research on language and communication differences between the genders.

In my own marketing research, I have seen that men and women communicate differently and respond to different verbiage.

Here's a comparison of male vs. female communication style:

MALE	FEMALE
Direct	Indirect/Polite
Competition	Cooperation
Highlight differences	Look for similarities
Transmit information	Form connections
Goal oriented	Relationship oriented
Key points	All her criteria
Facts and features	Stories and details
Credentials	Values
Solve problems	Share problems

Men are direct — Women are indirect

Men give and often prefer a short direct answer to their questions. Women tend to give longer answers as they provide background context for their answer. They are giving you information they think you need in order to fully understand their situation.

Women often express preferences as suggestions. Instead of saying, "I'd like to eat Italian," they might say, "Would you like to eat Italian tonight?" They also tend to be more polite, asking "Would you?" or "Could you?" Because of this, they appear more indirect and are sometimes viewed as being less decisive.

ACTION STEPS:

* Listen closely to what she says. She may be asking for something she wants/needs but doing it indirectly.
* If she appears to get off track, listen to see if she's really just giving you background information that will help answer your question.
* If you really are running out of time, look for opportunities to direct her back to your original questions. In the case of Sandra, when the wife asked about Sandra's job, Sandra could reply, "There are lots of things I love about my job. I'd be happy to sit down with you over coffee, and we can talk about career opportunities. For today, I just need your current salary. We can always make adjustments if your job situation changes."

Men look for differences — Women look for similarities

Men live in a hierarchical world. They are constantly looking for ways to separate themselves from the pack and gain a competitive edge. Women focus on a world of cooperation. They are constantly looking for ways to point out commonalities.

A great way to build rapport with women is to find shared values, situations and interests. I talked with one woman whose deciding factor in choosing her financial advisor was that he coached his daughter's softball team. She said, "That told me he cares about raising strong daughters. I knew this was someone I could trust."

ACTION STEP:

✳ Spend time talking about her life, family and values, and share your own experiences. You may not want to waste time on this "small talk," but it could be the difference between whether you get her business or not.

Men are focused on numbers — Women are focused on relationships

Men focus on numbers, performance, prices, returns, premiums, payouts and ROI. Women care about those things, too. But she also wants to know how all those things affect her, her family and the people she cares about. She cares not only about her relationships with her family, but also her relationship with you.

In an Oppenheimer Funds Women and Investing survey, they found that 73% of women surveyed who changed their financial advisors said they did so because their advisors did not understand them.[1]

The number one thing most women want from a financial professional is a long-term relationship. It's even more important than returns. Women want to know you understand their individual situation. They want a personal connection with you.

ACTION STEP:

✳ In your client communication (which she wants more of by the way), in addition to reviewing statements, do a life review. Find out what's going on with her and her family. Have there been any illnesses in the family? Does she have a dream to start her own business? Is she about to become a grandmother? Not only are you building a relationship, you're also identifying financial needs that can lead to more business.

This is also how you build trust. You'll learn more about that in Chapter 6 — How to Sell to Women.

Men want key facts — Women want detailed, rich stories

Numbers are powerful. We all like them (especially when they're big numbers). But when women share information, they tend to do it with stories and anecdotes.

While he may want to just get to the point, she may want to share and gather more information. Stories are a great way to share and convey important information and product benefits.

Use stories about other clients (obviously without sharing private details), and as a bonus, use a story that will also give her personal insight into your life. Do you have a story about what you learned about money from a parent? A value a relative passed to you? A story about your kids?

My financial advisor, Peter Walls, uses a story about golfing with his son to explain relative returns. "Some money managers or funds brag about beating the market average. But is that necessarily good? It's all about relativity. Relative to my 6-year-old son, I'm a pretty good golfer. But if I play with my dad, I'm a pretty lousy golfer. If a money manager beat the market, he claims he did well. But if the market was down 36% and he was only down 32%, is that good for you?"

ACTION STEPS:

✳ For every product you sell, have stories of how that product has affected your clients' lives. Stories are a great way to explain how a product works. And by the way, men love stories, too.

✳ If you can share some personal information in the story, that's even better for making an emotional connection with women clients.

Men look at your credentials — Women look at your values

This is incredibly important for women who are financial professionals. We talked earlier about how women want a personal relationship and connection with their advisor. (Remember the advisor who coaches his daughter's softball team.) It's important that women know what your values are. But female financial professionals also need to understand how important it is to state their credentials in order to win the confidence of men.

Women may have an advantage when it comes to relationship building, but they're not as bold about promoting their track record, expertise, awards and abilities.

If you're a female financial professional, find ways to share your credentials. I know a female advisor who brings her superior into prospective client meetings. The superior simply pops his head in the door and tells the prospective couple, "Ann here is one of our top people. I know she's going to do a terrific job for you." Just that one statement of confidence from an authority figure helped Ann close more new clients. (Guys, this can work for you as well.)

We'll go into this more in depth in Chapter 7 — How to Sell to Couples. You can also find more information on mistakes women make when selling to men at www.SellingFinancialServicesTo Women.com.

ACTION STEPS:

✳ For female producers in particular, list out reasons why you are competent and talented at what you do. Find a way to state those credentials upfront in client meetings (or have someone state it for you.)

✳ Let your clients know if you are up to date on the latest regulations, rules, Pension Protection Act, etc. Let your clients know of any training, courses or meetings you've attended to let them know you're on top of what's happening in the financial field.

Men want to solve problems — Women want to share problems

This is a biggie. I know as financial professionals it is your job to solve problems. But women bond by sharing and listening to each other's problems. They are often looking for a sounding board, a friendly ear. One of women's biggest complaints is that men don't listen to them, that men jump in too quickly and try to solve the problem for them.

When a woman is sharing a story/problem with you, she is giving you background information she thinks you need in order to truly understand her and her situation.

ACTION STEPS:

✳ Give her a chance to articulate her problem before you jump in and try to solve it. Until she's had a chance to tell you the full story, she won't have confidence in your recommendation.

✳ Continue to use the sales pitches you know are effective, but tack on an extra 15 minutes to half hour of just listening before you launch into them. You'll close more business.

CONCLUSION:

Men and women have different communication styles. (Note that many women in the financial industry actually have a more male communication style.) We can all do a better job of learning to speak each other's language. Communication is the key to persuasion. Persuasion is the key to more sales.

In order to be more persuasive, you need a deep understanding of the differences in how men and women look at money.

HOW MEN AND WOMEN
LOOK AT MONEY

In the book by Scott West and Mitch Anthony, *Storyselling for Financial Advisors — How Top Producers Sell,* an advisor describes how men and women feel about money, "My women clients tend to view their assets as a static pool of water that will eventually be depleted. My men seem to view it as a dynamic river of assets that keeps flowing."[1]

That's one of the better descriptions I've heard. In my research, men tend to look at money as something that ebbs and flows; it goes up and down. But there are always ways to make your money grow. Women tend to look at money as a set amount that's depleted every year until it's gone.

Perhaps it's because men have traditionally been the primary breadwinners, more secure in their ability to earn and generate income. This is changing quickly, but it could be a factor, especially for older women.

Here's a side by side look at how men and women look at money:

MEN	WOMEN
Protector/provider	Not dependent
Status	Security
Numbers	What can those numbers do for her

MEN	WOMEN
Opportunities	Consequences
Products	Plans
Credentials	Trust
Make it grow	Longevity — make it last
River that rises and falls	Set amount that's depleted 'til it's gone

One of the biggest takeaways from this comparison is how much women focus on having a comprehensive plan. Men, with their more compartmentalized brains, may focus on a single goal. "We're here today to buy life insurance." "This meeting is to discuss my IRA." "Today let's look at our quarterly report to see how much money we're making/losing."

Women, with their more holistic brains, want to broaden out the conversation. "Today we're talking about life insurance, but what else do we need as part of the plan if something happens to us? Who gets custody of the kids if we're both gone? What do we need to have in our wills? What happens to my business if I'm no longer around? Do I need to have a succession plan?"

Men tend to look at this line of thinking as "getting off track." But broadening out the conversation can work to your advantage since it helps you identify more selling opportunities. It works to her advantage since she can give you the information and context she believes you need in order to understand her unique situation.

The importance of his provider status

NOTE TO WIVES: Never underestimate how strongly your husband feels about his provider status. I know a fairly affluent couple. They are involved in many philanthropic ventures. The wife has a habit of saying, "We don't have a lot of money, but we contribute what we can." Every time she says this, I see her husband's face fall.

Wives, never comment in front of your husband, "We don't have a lot of money." How would you feel if he said, "We're not good parents," or "We eat out because we're too lazy to cook," or hit one of your other sensitive buttons. You'd take it personally. And believe me, he takes it personally as well.

Men WANT to be terrific providers. It's one of the reasons why they focus so much on returns. Yes, it's a status thing, but it's also a provider thing. Combine this with his higher risk tolerance, and you see the attractiveness of taking more chances if there's an opportunity to hit it big.

As one advisor told me, "Men are looking to hit home runs. They're willing to strike out a few times if it means slamming one out of the park. Women are more focused on hitting singles. They just keep hitting singles 'til they eventually score a run."

Because there can be widely divergent investment strategies and risk tolerances, it's important to get men and women on the same page when making financial decisions. We'll go into this in depth in Chapter 7 — How to Sell to Couples.

ACTION STEPS:

* ✳ Even if you are selling a single product (life insurance) have the broader discussion. You may find opportunities to sell more products yourself or refer a partner (lawyer, business strategist, etc.).
* ✳ Tie product benefits to his provider and protector roles.
* ✳ Tie product benefits to her fear that she will run out of money.

Women's financial priorities

When it comes to women's financial lives, what do they care about the most? In my Women and Finance Survey we asked women questions about how they view money and financial planning. Here are the answers:

What financial issues are you most concerned about?

Women under 50:

1. Feeling financially secure
2. Retirement planning
3. Getting out of debt
4. Having a comprehensive plan in place

Women over 50:

1. Feeling financially secure
2. Having a comprehensive plan in place
3. Retirement planning
4. Outliving your money

It's interesting to note that women under 50 are very concerned about getting out of debt. Women over 50 are concerned about outliving their money

What does having money allow you to do?

Women under 50:

1. Provide for your family
2. Take care of yourself and the people you love

Women over 50:

1. Take care of yourself and people you love
2. Not have to rely on others

We saw big differences between the under and over 50 groups on this question. Women under 50 rated "provide for your family" way higher than the women over 50. This may reflect our earlier stats about the earning power of women. Younger women may be coming in with different expectations of their role as a breadwinner (or at least contributor) and provider.

For the over 50 women, not having to rely on others was way more important to them than the under 50 crowd.

Both groups are very focused on family and the people they love. While men can focus on money (status, numbers, power), women focus on how that money affects their family and loved ones.

ACTION STEPS:

* In conversations with women under 50, focus on how you can help them reduce their debt. Warning, do not say anything that sounds judgmental.
* In conversations with women over 50, focus on ways you can help them make sure they won't outlive their money. (Hint: annuities)
* Talk about how your products can help women of all ages take care of themselves and the people they love. This will require asking questions about who those people are, another reason to have that "small talk" about family and people who are important in your clients' lives.
* If you're talking about a number, say a life insurance death benefit, don't just throw out a number. Tie that number to an affect on a family member. For instance, her son could use the money to pay off his mortgage or the amount could go to pay for her grandkids' college.
* For women under 50, ask about all the ways in which they are responsible for their families. Do not assume responsibility for providing is the sole domain of the husband. (Hint: life insurance for her)

✳ For women over 50, talk about how your products can help them avoid situations where they have to rely on others. (Hint: long-term care insurance)

CONCLUSION:

Men and women can approach money and financial decisions from different directions. Understand the priorities and concerns that matter most to both men and women. Make sure you approach the selling process from her point of view as well as his. What is her point of view? Let's look at that next.

HOW TO SELL
TO WOMEN

Remember the story in the introduction to the book about the financial advisor and the widow? He knew she had some of her money with him, but knew there was more out there. He couldn't seem to gain enough of the widow's confidence to play a bigger role in her financial planning.

After attending the seminar, he applied what he learned, including enhanced listening skills and relationship building techniques (which we'll talk about in a moment) with his female clients, including the aforementioned widow. The widow transferred her entire portfolio to this advisor to the tune of 20 million dollars.

How do you win 20 million dollars worth of trust? How can you increase your book of business? How can you get more business from your existing clients? Read on.

Three tips on selling to women

Meet Judy Hoberman, President and author of *Selling In A Skirt*. Judy specializes in uncovering the obvious and not so obvious differences between men and women when it comes to selling and recruiting. She shares her insight on what to do and what not to do when selling to women.

Everyone has their idea of what is expected from a salesperson the first time you meet them: They need to be knowledgeable about the product or service they are offering; they need to be professional; and they need to be on time and bring value . . . meaning they should have done their homework on the potential client. While all of this is true, women expect that and a little more. Women also need to build a relationship with the salesperson, the company that person represents and the product or service they are offering. Women also want all their questions answered, no matter how trivial they might seem. Finally they want to be heard and listened to. Listening is the key to selling and is one of the most important aspects of the sales process.

Case in point: Early in my career, one of my first sales positions was with a burglar alarm company. During my training, I was told not to ask any questions about how the alarm worked because it was such a "simple" process. And I was assured that the clients wouldn't ask any questions, either. This is what I was told, "Just demonstrate the product, and it will sell itself. Don't ask them what they want or need. Have the 'package' put together, and get in and out. You will be dealing with the husband, and he wants to protect his family."

I was young and new to the job, so I followed my trainer's instructions. I arrived at the client's home, walked in, introduced myself and proceeded to set up the alarm. I was stopped dead in my tracks by the female client, who immediately started asking me question after question: "How does it work? Is it connected to the police? Why is this alarm different than others? How many customers does the alarm company have? Could you provide me with some referrals of happy customers?" I couldn't believe the number of questions she had, but I did my best to answer them, even though I hadn't been prepared for those questions during my training.

Two hours later, the appointment ended and my clients said they needed to think about the product and would let me know their decision the next morning. When I returned to the office, my manager told me that I must have done something wrong to prompt all those questions and to have not made the sale. The female client asked those questions because she wanted to establish rapport with me and with the product I was selling. She knew I heard her concerns and listened to the reasons behind them.

By the way, I completed that sale and earned her trust and many referrals to boot.

Knowing these simple things will give you some advantages in the sales arena. Unfortunately, not everyone will heed this advice so here are three mistakes many sales people make when meeting a woman for the first time:

1 — Not taking the time to build a relationship. Women need to build a relationship first. They are buying you in addition to your product/service. The more you focus on understanding their problems, the more they will trust that you are the one they should work with. Position your product/service in terms of how it fits into her life by focusing on her rather than on the features and benefits of the product.

2 — Assuming you know what is best for her. You don't necessarily know everything your prospect needs. Leave your assumptions behind and keep an open mind. No question is too simple or "obvious" to answer. Give her the opportunity to ask as many questions as she wants, and answer them all. Don't rush to provide a solution before you understand the true need.

3 — Ignoring her listening style and assuming the close. To a woman, good listening skills include making eye contact and reacting visually to whomever is speaking. When a woman nods, it means she is listening and is engaged. It doesn't mean that she agrees with what is being said nor is it a signal to proceed. A woman listens and takes in the information to build rapport and relationships, and isn't that the ultimate goal?

I love Judy's story for so many reasons. You've all probably been through sales training that focused on the same thing — get in and out with as little conversation as possible. It's all about closing the sale in that first meeting. Yet this training can backfire on male and female professionals.

Women have questions they want answered. As noted in Judy's story, women may feel like it's OK to ask more questions when dealing with another woman. This is a good thing! If she has questions and concerns, it's better to get them out in the open than to have her say nothing and torpedo the sale behind your back.

Be the quarterback of her team

Judy mentioned the importance of building relationships. When your female clients need trusted advice, are you the person they call? Your female clients likely have a team of professionals they work with: an accountant, estate attorney, insurance agent, financial advisor. Ideally, all of these people would work together to take care of all her needs. And she's looking for someone to be the quarterback, to be the one person she trusts the most to lead that team. Be that person. Be the quarterback.

The quarterback of her team is going to have the most influence and likely the most loyalty. How do you get the quarterback position? By having the best understanding of her whole situation.

For example, an affluent widow needed to figure out how to split the inheritance between her two children. Her daughter was very attentive, visited often and took care of her after her surgery. They were very close. Her son rarely ever called or visited. She wanted to leave more money to her daughter. She was thinking of splitting it 2/3 for her daughter, 1/3 for her son.

She had a lawyer who would draw up the will, but her financial advisor was the quarterback of her team. He was the one she went to for advice on what to do. She asked for his opinion and for alternate solutions she could consider. He pointed to a potential rift between the siblings with her current solution, but made it clear it was all about her wishes. The widow didn't want to do anything to harm her children's relationship. She decided she would leave the house to her daughter. Her daughter loved the house, and her son had shown no interest in it. Then she could split the rest 50/50.

Was this the perfect solution? Who knows. But it was a solution the widow felt was comfortable and fair. THIS is how you build trust. THIS is how you generate referrals — by having the broader, deeper conversations, by understanding her whole situation and by being the trusted quarterback of her team.

ACTION STEPS:

* Have a team of experts ready to refer to your client. She may ask you to recommend an accountant or lawyer. This allows you to work with people you trust, and provides cross referral partnerships.
* Ask questions that show you are interested. Understand her whole situation. (For a great list of questions, read Chapter 13 — The Client Meeting — Women-Winning Questions)
* Tell her she can come to you with any questions. Most clients respect your time and won't take advantage of this. Be her most trusted advisor and you will have more influence, gain her trust and loyalty and generate more referrals.

The undisputed power of listening

Here's one of the single most important things you'll learn in this book, the Holy Grail of selling to women — it's the power of listening.

You all have sales techniques that work for you — a certain way you describe a product, a killer closing technique, an amazing way to address a common objection. I'm not asking you to change techniques that you know work for you. But I am asking you to add in extra listening time to your sales presentations. Here's why...

One of women's biggest complaints is that financial professionals don't have their client's best needs at heart. Many people still feel financial professionals are just out for the highest commission. How do you combat that? How do you let someone know you care about their needs? By listening to them! By taking the time to ask questions and really find out what those needs are. (Hint: asking a few high level questions about financial goals isn't going to cut it.)

Women are interrupted twice as often as men. What message do you send when you interrupt someone? *What I have to say is more important. I don't care about what you think. Enough about you, let's get back to me.* Interrupting is a sign of lack of interest and lack of respect. When you don't interrupt, women notice, big time. It's not always conscious, but they walk out of the meeting thinking, "I just have a good feeling about this person."

You don't build trust by talking, you build trust by listening. Now I know I'm getting some pushback from you. *"But if I can just share my knowledge and expertise and track record, I know they'll trust me enough to do business with me."* Yes, sharing your credentials is essential. But with women, trust is earned by listening. Our financial advisor didn't win 20 million dollars by talking. He didn't say anything different. He added in more listening. He didn't talk more, he actually talked less.

For those of you out there who think you're great listeners, here's something to think about, 49 out of every 60 seconds the financial broker is doing the talking.[1]

Here's the most beautiful thing about winning trust by listening — when clients trust you, you can do your best work. Clients who trust you:

* Take up less of your time
* Accept more of your recommendations
* Remain loyal even during market downturns

Listening Test — Three Questions

How important is listening to women? Ask them!

When promoting Genworth Financial's Connecting with Women Clients seminar, Genworth's Kevin Riley meets with male financial producers in their office and asks them to gather some of their female co-workers. Kevin has the male producer ask these women three questions:

1. What if when you came to me with any questions or concerns, I listened intently, made eye contact and understood the importance of my attention to you?
2. What if I didn't offer a solution until you'd fully articulated the problem and were done talking? I would only chime in to make sure I was on the same page as you or make sure I heard you correctly.
3. What if, when you are talking to me, I did not let other things take importance over what you are saying? No interruptions, looking at my computer, taking calls or looking over your shoulder at other things that are happening.

When the male producer asks these questions of female co-workers, the answer is always the same . . .

The women laugh out loud and say, "That will never happen."

So Kevin follows up with the women, "But what if he did? Would it make this a better place to work and improve your relationships?"

The answer is always an unequivocal "Yes!"

Kevin then turns to the male producer and says, "This is what we'll teach you and your agents in the Connecting with Women seminar."

Do this now: Go up to any woman in your office, or in your family, and ask her the above three questions. Go ahead. I'll wait.

So, what was the response?

Even if you think you're a great listener, do the listening test above. You may be surprised by the answers.

Four listening techniques that grow trust and close sales

It's easy to say, "Be a better listener," but it's not easy to do. So here are four techniques you can use to improve your listening skills, gain trust and close more sales.

1 — The power of the pause.

You see someone talking then they pause, scratch their chin, look up at the ceiling, say, "um..." They are thinking! You've asked a question that's important enough for them to really think about their answer. You are about to get a golden nugget of information. It is SO hard not to jump in and fill that pause. But don't. Shut up. Give them the time to gather and express their thought. If you jump in, you may cause them to lose track of what they were going to say. Even worse, don't try to finish their thought for them. Let me know how that works out for you.

Sit with the pause. Don't jump in. Wait to hear what comes next.

2 — WAIT = Why Am I Talking?

Put a sticky note by your phone or computer that says "WAIT" an acronym for Why Am I Talking. This is a reminder to make sure you aren't hogging most of the time on the call. State what you need to say, then give the floor to your client and listen to their thoughts, feelings and opinions.

By the way, this isn't important just for women, it's important for men as well. I've been at many meetings where male clients talk about their financial service provider and how much it means to them that their provider listens to them.

3 — Give less advice, ask better questions

This is one of the most valuable sales techniques I ever learned. It has had a huge impact on my business and personal life. When I'm in a sales situation, I make sure my credentials are stated up front — I bring a copy of my book, give specifics on the services I provide, let them know the big name companies I work with — but all this takes less than a minute. Then I start asking questions.

Speaking engagement example:

When I'm selling my seminars or speaking services, I always ask about the audience. Who will be attending? What are their biggest challenges? What types of speakers have they responded to? What do they NOT want to hear? Most of the call is spent on learning who the audience is, what their goals are and what the goals of the sponsoring organization are.

I rarely lose a sale. Yes, I'm good at what I do and at differentiating myself, but the number one reason why I close so many sales is because I ask really good questions. I am not a natural sales person. But I am focused on delivering positive results. And to do that you have to know your audience and what they want. My clients feel like I truly understand their business, their challenges and their goals.

Here's a testimonial from a bank for whom I did a presentation:

"Holly, thank you for enhancing your exceptional presentation with (bank name) retail themes. My teammates were impressed with your research information and willingness to customize your delivery for our team. We look forward to future engagements. Tami."

Long-term care example:

Here's an example for selling long-term care insurance. You have a client with an aging parent. The client has expressed an interest in learning if they should purchase long-term care insurance for that parent. You could give lots and lots of advice and information about long-term care policies.

But first, ask them questions that will help lead them to that decision themselves.

- "If your parent did deteriorate, who would provide the care?"
- "Who would be responsible for paying for that care?"
- "Do you know how much that care would cost?"
- "What's your parent's biggest fear?" (If it's being placed in a nursing home, you know you can stress in-home benefits.)

You get the idea. Instead of rattling off a bunch of stats, you're engaging the client, asking questions, listening and demonstrating that you care about the client's unique situation.

4 — Let her articulate her problem before you jump in and try to solve it

A man's wife comes home from work. She shares a story of a problem she's having with her boss. She is thoroughly frustrated. Her husband jumps in with pieces of advice on how she can handle her boss and suggestions about what she can say. She bristles at his advice. When he finally offers, "Well if it's that bad, why don't you just quit?" he is met with disbelief by his wife.

"Quit my job? I can't do that!" she says as she gives him the evil eye.

Loving husbands everywhere walk away from these encounters feeling confused at best, unappreciated at worst. He's trying to help her solve a problem, yet all she does is rebuke his suggestions.

One of the ways women reduce stress is to talk about what's bothering them. The best way to bond with them is to just listen and let them get it all out. With all those connections to the verbal centers of her brain, the act of simply talking and expressing her feelings makes her feel better.

The most important thing is that she shares the problem, NOT that you fix the problem. Listening and providing empathy is the key to success. Yes, as a financial professional it is your job to solve problems, but let your clients articulate their problems fully before you go into problem-solving mode.

Fathers of teenage daughters everywhere understand the power of this skill. When your daughter comes home distressed, ask her what's up, then simply sit back and listen. You can add in a few comments here and there, "Wow, he said that?" "Really, that's what she thinks?" "For real?" But do NOT try to solve her problem straight off. Simply let her share her feelings about what happened. If she wants your opinion on what she should do, she'll ask for it.

I've talked to a surprising amount of men who've said this technique has worked wonders with their wives and their daughters.

In a sales situation, this technique works just as well. Let her articulate her problem, her concerns and share her stories. Once she is finished sharing, NOW you can offer solutions. That is, after all, what you are hired to do. But listen first. Even if you know within three minutes of her walking in the door what she needs, listen anyways. And close more sales.

Scenario — female client upset about a big drop in the market

You get a call from a woman who is severely stressed by the recent dramatic drop in the stock market. You could:

1. Share information about how the market is cyclical and its historical performance. (Least effective approach. This will do little to address her fear and panic. You'll probably hear from her again with the exact same problem.)
2. Go over the plan you have in place and remind her of her long-term goals. (Better, though you still haven't let her articulate what her true fears/problems are.)
3. Ask her to share her concerns with you. Let her articulate her fears. Then use tactics 1 and 2. (Best option. By letting her share her concerns and problems, you're getting to the root cause of her fear. By listening, you're building trust and demonstrating a desire to truly understand her unique situation. Now, when it's your turn to talk, you can use solution 1 and 2, and tie those solutions to her specific fears.)

If you choose option 3, you will likely not hear from her again since she's had a chance to truly articulate her fears. If you go with option 1 or 2, get ready for more panicked phone calls.

Women want to be not only listened to but heard. Repeat back key points to make sure you've understood her correctly.

ACTION STEPS:

* Use the power of the pause. Don't interrupt.
* Listen more, talk less. Use the listening techniques above.
* Ask better questions. Even if you think you know the answer, ask the question before you jump in with your thoughts and opinions.
* Don't jump right in and try to solve her problem. Let her articulate it first.

Address her concerns and objections

Most sales people look at objections as problems to be overcome. This is a dangerous approach to take with women. Women often complain that their objections and concerns aren't taken seriously.

If she has an objection, empathize with her. Do not try to play down or invalidate her concern.

Scenario 1:
An advisor is talking to a female client about a mutual fund he's recommending she purchase. The client mentions that she's concerned about what would happen if the stock market were to take a big dive. She's afraid the mutual fund would lose a great deal of its value.

The advisor talks about market cycles and how, historically, the market has outperformed other vehicles, and that a mutual fund, with a variety of stocks, is less risky than investing in single stocks.

But the client still hesitates. The advisor wonders why women are so risk averse that they won't take good advice.

Scenario 2:

An advisor is talking to a female client about a mutual fund he's recommending she purchase. The client mentions that she's concerned about what would happen if the stock market were to take a big dive. She's afraid the mutual fund would lose a great deal of its value.

The advisor asks if she has been in that situation before. He acknowledges that he has other clients that had a similar fear. He asks about her concerns. He explains the portions of her retirement plan that are designed to provide protection in just such a scenario. THEN he says everything the advisor said in scenario one.

By acknowledging her objection and concerns, letting her talk about her fear and validating her concern by telling her other clients have the same concern, you are gaining her trust. Once you have her trust, you will find she accepts your recommendations more easily.

Techno-jargon check

Financial professionals want to display their expertise. It's a way of establishing hierarchy. "I have knowledge and experience that you don't, so you should hire me." Demonstrating this knowledge by using a lot of technical terms with your clients can backfire big time with women (and with some men). Women say they think financial professionals use technical language to purposefully try to make them feel stupid.

If you use a technical term, explain it in plain English. But be aware — there are some terms you use so often, you've forgotten the average person does not understand them.

I don't know what it is with folks in the financial industry, but you all just love your acronyms. "I was recently at the NAIFA meeting talking with a bunch of CFP's talking about what's new with VA's, REIT's and ETF's and how the PPA is going to change the way we look at the LTC industry." Seriously, you should listen to yourselves some time. Many people won't know what you're talking about, but will be afraid to speak up for fear of looking stupid.

ACTION STEP:

✳ Have a woman who is not in the industry read over your materials or listen to your investment strategy/product description. Have her call you out whenever you say something she doesn't understand. It will be an eye-opening experience.

Women want a long-term relationship

According to a Genworth consumer segmentation study, 78% of women said that building long-term relationships with financial institutions is more important than always getting the best prices or newest products.[2]

Some financial professionals look at sales as *transactional*. It's a numbers game. Get as many people in the pipeline as you can, close them as fast as possible and move on. Others look at sales as *relational*. They take the time to build relationships. They really get to know their customers and clients. It's no surprise that women prefer the relational model. Remember, female brains focus on similarities and values. One of their biggest complaints about sales people is that:

1. Sales people move in too fast for the close.
2. The sales person didn't take the time to truly understand her unique situation.

If you do take the time to really listen, get to know her and her individual situation and build a relationship, you win her loyalty. (Can you say client retention?) And you win her trust, which leads directly to more business and referrals.

Women want more communication

In my Women and Finance Survey, I asked the following question:

If you could change one thing about the way you work with your financial advisor, what would it be?

Here's a sample of the answers:

> *He would offer more services than just selling products*
> *I want more personal contact so that he understands my life and priorities*
> *I would be in touch with him more often*
> *More opportunities for check-in*
> *I would like to see him more often*
> *That he check in with us more often*
> *Don't meet with her enough*
> *More regular communication*
> *More contact throughout the year*
> *Regularly scheduled meetings to discuss plans*
> *I would discuss more things with him*
> *More time to meet with her*
> *More interaction*
> *We'd have personalized conversations on a more regular basis*
> *I would like more touch points with my advisor*

Hmmmmm, notice a pattern here?

By FAR the most consistent answer to what women would change about the way they work with their financial advisor would be to have more communication.

Here's the problem. You already have a full busy schedule. How can you provide more communication? First, look at your most important clients, your top 20%. Focus on them first. Look at personal touch points you can set up: lunch, coffee, a phone call to check-in, an increase in the number of reviews and updates you have with them. Ask yourself these questions:

- How often do we meet face-to-face?
- How many phone calls do we have in a year?

- How often do we schedule updates where I can sit down and discuss what changes are occurring in their lives as well as their portfolios?
- How often do I talk to the wife, or are the vast majority of conversations with the husband only?

This last one is a biggie. We'll look at this further in Chapter 7 — How to Sell to Couples.

Communicate more often — Develop more touch points

What about the rest of your clients? There are several ways to have mass contact that don't require a lot of time on your part:

- Regular email updates
- Customer appreciation events
- Greeting cards — I know it sounds hokey, but today cards in the mail are rare and thus genuinely appreciated. Send out a birthday card with a Starbucks gift card. It doesn't need to be a huge amount. She will appreciate that you reached out and will think fondly of you while she's ordering a latte. If she's with a friend she may even remark about the kind gift from her advisor.
- Celebrate achievements — I talked with an advisor who had a female client who was retiring. He threw a retirement lunch for her and 10 of her friends. Her friends were amazed, commenting that their advisors would never do anything like that. The advisor who threw the lunch walked away with new business without doing a single sales pitch.
- Provide solidarity during rough times. Hopefully you're in touch often enough to know if someone is ill or has died. Attend funerals. Seriously. Weddings are where you find out who your acquaintances are. Funerals are where you find out who your friends are.

Speaking of funerals, what is the number one thing people want to do after they've lost someone they love? They want to talk about that person.

My friend Mary's father passed away. While making funeral arrangements, her mother commented that she wanted to find a new financial advisor. (Remember that stat — 7 out of 10 women leave their financial advisors within three years of divorcing or widowing). Mary was shocked. Her mother and father had been with the same advisor for decades. But right before the funeral, the advisor came over and talked to Mary's mom and told her how much her husband meant to him and shared stories of their time together. He got emotional remembering how Mary's father had given him his first big chance — her dad was the advisor's first big client. Well, after that, Mary's mom decided to give the advisor another chance. He finally made an emotional connection with her. And he'll never know how close he came to losing one of his biggest accounts.

ACTION STEPS:

* Review your biggest accounts. Is it a couple? Make sure you have a relationship with the wife. How hard would it be to replace that money if something happened to him and she went to another advisor?
* Communicate more often and in-person with your top clients. Identify your top 20% and make sure you're having regular contact, including face-to-face meetings with no objective other than to just find out what's going on in their lives.
* Increase the number of touch points you have with your clients including email updates, greeting cards, customer appreciation events, etc. Be there to help them celebrate and to help them grieve. For more ideas on how to communicate more often with your clients, visit www.SellingFinancialServicesToWomen.com.

Share information about yourself

Relationships are two-way streets. Yes, I just spent practically a whole chapter on the importance of listening. It is vitally important that you spend more time listening than talking. But it is also important to share some of your personal information. Remember, women are looking for ways in which you are like them. They want to know who you are and what your values are. They want to know if you are someone who deserves their trust.

I told you about the woman who chose her financial advisor because he coached his daughter's softball team. That sent her a message that he cared about raising strong daughters.

I met an insurance agent who wears the most gaudy, truly atrocious ties I've ever seen. I asked him about it and he said his grandkids have a contest every Christmas to see who can buy him the ugliest tie. He then proudly wears those ties to work. They are always great conversation starters. And how do you not love a guy who wears awful ties in order to make his grandkids happy?

I worked with a lawyer several years back who sent out a monthly newsletter and always included a personal story in every one. No, these weren't tales of ski trips to Aspen (always be cautious when sharing family vacations that can appear lavish.) He shared stories about the adventures of adopting a rescue dog, about a lesson his daughter taught him about when it's time to put down work and pay attention to your family. He shared a favorite quote and why it inspired him. What surprised him was that almost all of his clients brought up those stories in meetings and how often a story would lead to very meaningful conversations. (Can you say relationship building?)

If you meet clients in your office, find ways to let your office tell your story. Here's a test: Ask any woman what the first thing is that she looks at when entering an office. I bet you nine times out of ten she says, "family photographs." Put photos front and center. Have a wall calendar that conveys one of your passions. Display a favorite quote. Have a shelf of books you like to read. Women will notice.

They're desperately searching for ways to find common ground with you. Help them out.

Women also visit your website and look at your bio. (We'll talk more about websites in Chapter 11 — Marketing Financial Services to Women.) This is a HUGE missed opportunity for most financial professionals. Yes, I understand your bio needs to sound professional. Talk about your education and training and years of experience. But also look for ways you can add a personal or unexpected touch.

Shari Storm is the Vice President and Marketing Manager at Verity Credit Union. Shari uses a different bio depending on the site. For the main site, she has a buttoned up professional bio. But for the Our Voices by Verity Credit Union blog, she shares more personal information including, "Most people would never know that I am obsessed with music (I just hit 30,000 songs in iTunes), that I once had a body guard or that I worked at a nuclear reactor for two years." After reading that bio, is Shari a more interesting person to you? Does she feel more like a real person? And how many conversation starters do you now have: music obsession, body guard and nuclear reactor.

I know many of you may be limited on what you can put in your bio. But try to add at least something that gives people a glimpse into who you are and what really matters to you. (Hint: What is one thing about you that most people would never guess?)

Bottom line: Be authentic, make a real connection, surprise people (in a good way) and be memorable.

This is especially effective in networking situations or when you are providing a bio for a speaking engagement. It gives people something to walk up and talk to you about.

Women, this can be especially powerful for you. Many in the industry will try to stereotype you. What about you would surprise co-workers or prospective clients?

I know a fiery young red-headed female business owner who, when describing herself, includes the fact that she has an almost photographic memory of baseball statistics. Her father was an avid fan, and since he didn't have a son, he shared his passion with his daughter. Sharing this information does two things: One, it provides common ground with other sports enthusiasts. Two, it changes people's perception that she's a lightweight "girly girl." (Her words, not mine.)

I watched an attractive financial professional present to a room full of men. They were sort of paying attention, until she said something that made every one of them sit up and take notice. She shared that she spent 10 years in the military repairing helicopters. Talk about breaking through stereotypes. The men looked at her with new admiration.

For more suggestions on how women can gain credibility with men, visit www.SellingFinancialServicesToWomen.com.

ACTION STEPS:

* Share information about yourself. Decorate your office with personal items, wear a lapel pin with your favorite cause, wear a crazy tie or interesting piece of jewelry or display a favorite quote.
* Include personal information in your bio. Share something specific about yourself that will convey who you are and what matters to you.
* Be memorable. Share something specific that most people don't know about you that can be a conversation starter.

Educate her

When I talk to financial producers, they often tell me that the wife simply doesn't want to participate in the financial conversations and decision making. Beware. I've surveyed many women who say, "Why would I want to go into a meeting where the advisor is just going to throw around a bunch of technical jargon and spend the whole time talking to my husband?"

Sometimes women don't participate because they are expecting a bad experience. Do not mistake this to mean they aren't a part of the decision making process.

In my Women and Finance Survey, I asked the question, **"If you could change one thing about the way you work with your financial advisor, what would it be?"** We saw earlier that more communication was the top answer. But more education was also a popular theme with answers like:

> *He would give better explanations*
> *I would have more knowledge about investing*
> *I would put more time into educating myself*
> *Less jargon in his advice*
> *More explanation about alternative options*
> *Understand the logistics of the trading that is done*
> *I'd like more knowledge*
> *I'd like more access to ask quick questions*
> *He'd help me make more smart decisions*

Educate her and make her feel confident

Talking the lingo is great if you're on CNBC, but in the confines of your office or your client's home, do everything you can to help them understand the advice you're giving.

Include simple, memorable descriptions. It's vitally important your clients be able to understand and articulate the financial decisions they are making for two reasons:

1. If they understand your recommendations, they are far more likely to have confidence in them.
2. If they can talk intelligently to their friends and family, they can share your expertise and create more chances for referrals.

This second reason is also especially important for women, not only for their referral potential, but also to combat one of the most frustrating problems financial professionals face — The Brother-In-Law Effect.

I already see heads nodding. You know what I'm talking about. You've spent a lot of time explaining why a certain product, let's say an annuity, would be a perfect fit for her. She seems convinced when she leaves your office, but she comes back the next week and says, "My brother-in-law says annuities are bad," and you lose the sale. (And she loses the opportunity to buy a valuable product that could really help her.)

How do you battle The Brother-In-Law Effect? By educating her, arming her with information and being up front about the pros and cons.

"You've told me that one of your biggest fears is outliving your money. So we can set up an annuity to provide you with guaranteed income for life. This way your basic expenses will be paid. Now, some people don't like annuities because they want an investment with a higher return. But that's not the job of this money. The job of this money is to let you sleep at night knowing you'll never run out of money. This other portion of your portfolio is for growth. Its job is to deliver a higher return."

By educating her and sharing the pros and the cons, she now has the knowledge and the language to stand up to her brother-in-law and not blindly accept his opinion. An empowered female investor is your best client.

Provide other educational opportunities

Educate her one-on-one, but also look for other opportunities to educate women, whether they are clients or prospective clients. Share your knowledge through speaking opportunities, training sessions and seminars.

Here are some possible seminar topics:

- How to teach kids about money
- How men and women can talk to each other about money (great for newlyweds as well as married couples)
- Sandwiched caregivers — who takes care of the caregiver?
- The four biggest mistakes in retirement planning
- Beyond the 401K — what you need to know about investing
- Financial planning for business owners
- The four financial keys to setting up a successful business
- Everything you always wanted to know but were afraid to ask your financial advisor
- Caring for aging parents — do you know what insurance your parents have?
- Are you over or under insured?
- The new health care law — how it will affect your financial planning
- How to get started when your financial life is in a shoe box
- The myth of Prince Charming — what young women need to know about financial planning
- Financial Security University
- How to stay on top of the stock market but still be able to sleep at night

The topics are endless. You all have some sort of expertise. It does not take much work to prepare a 30-minute talk, put together a Power Point presentation or simply stand up and answer questions from the crowd.

Do your own educational events and invite your clients. The price of admission is they must bring someone else with them. Women especially love to bring friends to these types of seminars. You are now in front of a room of highly qualified prospects. Learn more about client events in Chapter 9 — Referrals — How to Generate Word of Mouth.

For your female clients who like to read, there's a great book by Starr Cochran, *The Bread & Butter Chronicles*. It is a fictional look at a group of women in different life situations and how they handle their finances. It includes a widow, a divorcee and two married women. It is written for women, but men enjoy the book as well. Many women can relate to the situations in the book. I especially like this book because it's a fictional story that reads as a novel, but with financial learning added in. Have extra copies to hand out to your female clients. It can be a great conversation starter.

Remember, women are desperate for good financial advice. There's a reason why Suze Orman is one of the top rated shows on TV. Empower women and win their business.

ACTION STEPS:

✴ Educate your female clients about products and your investment strategies. If she can repeat what you say to someone else, it can increase referrals as well as her self-esteem and confidence in your recommendations.

✴ Avoid The Brother-In-Law Effect. Advise her of the pros and cons. Address objections head-on and give her the knowledge and language she needs to overcome those objections, both for herself and to others who may be trying to influence her decisions.

CONCLUSION:

Listening, asking better questions, providing more communication and education — these are all trust builders, and trust is what it's all about. Yes, you may have to spend more time with her, but she's worth it. Women want a long-term relationship. Once they have a good one, they don't want to leave. In tough times, when her husband isn't getting the returns he wants, she may be the voice of reason telling him to stay put and stick with the long-term plan.

Do everything you can to reach out to, inform and partner with women in their financial decision making. Do a good job with her, and watch other women march in your door.

Many of these women will bring their husbands with them. So it's important to know how to sell to couples.

HOW TO SELL TO COUPLES

When working with couples, have you noticed that they are often not on the same page financially?

Here's an example. I talked with an advisor who was working with the husband of a couple. The husband had $10,000 from a CD he wanted to invest elsewhere. The advisor and husband agreed to use that money to fund a long-term care policy. Everything was ready to go until the husband came back to the advisor and fessed up that his wife actually had a different plan for the money. Not only did the advisor lose a sale, the couple missed out on the all-important protection that a LTC policy would have provided.

It was all because the husband and wife weren't on the same page financially. But note, the other problem was the advisor's failure to make sure the wife was included in the meeting. (Was it also the husband's responsibility to include the wife? You bet. But as the advisor, you're in the driver's seat. Take control and set yourself up for success by including both spouses in the meeting.)

What should you do and not do when selling to couples? Here are six tips to help you connect with both spouses:

Tip #1 — Make sure both spouses are included in your meetings and in the decision making process

Tip #2 — Get them on the same page

Tip #3 — Respect different decision making styles

Tip #4 — Understand different investment timelines

Tip #5 — Understand his *"That won't happen to me"* mindset

Tip #6 — Watch your body language

Selling to Couples Tip #1 — Make sure both spouses are included in meetings and decision making

Think about it. Who can do a better job of selling a product or a financial plan or strategy, your client or you? Would you rather a husband go home and try to explain to his wife why a decision is a good idea, or would you rather have that opportunity yourself?

I know some of you are thinking, "But the husband (or wife) really is the decision maker. The other spouse really isn't interested." Both spouses don't need to be present at every meeting or on every phone call, but when major decisions are being made, you need to be in front of them both.

One way to approach this is to say, "John, I know you're the main decision maker, but these decisions are going to affect both of your financial futures. I want to bring Julie in just to make sure she understands the plan. Chances are she's going to outlive you, so it's important she knows what's going on. And this way, if she has any concerns, I can address them so you don't have to."

No husband wants to make a decision now, only to have it challenged later by his wife.

Remember that we're also seeing more wives taking the lead in financial decision making. In that case, it's important to bring the husband into the mix.

In the meeting, make sure you are giving equal attention to both spouses. Shake hands with both. Give both of them your business card. Ask questions and make eye-contact with both the husband and the wife.

Be aware that in public, some women may let their husbands take the lead. It looks like he is the main decision maker. But when they get home in private, the wife actually has a strong voice in the final decision. So don't make assumptions. Go into every meeting believing that both partners have a voice in the final decision.

ACTION STEPS:

* ✳ Include both spouses in important planning meetings.
* ✳ If the husband states he's the sole decision maker and his wife doesn't care to be included, emphasize the fact she may one day be responsible for the decision making and needs to understand the overall financial plan.
* ✳ Give equal attention to both. Shake both their hands, and give both of them your business card.

Selling to Couples Tip #2 — Get them on the same page

As we saw in the opening example, bad things happen when couples have different priorities, different investment styles, different concerns and different visions of what the future looks like.

These discussions can be difficult. This is where you need to put on your therapist hat and help your clients talk about money. The best way to do that is to ask open-ended questions about their goals and their concerns. (For specific questions, see Chapter 13 — The Client Meeting — Women-Winning Questions.)

Here's the story of a wife who is concerned about her husband's need to always pick up the check:

"My husband is the most generous person in the world. We're starting to get serious about retirement and realize we don't have the disposable income we used to have. My husband's charming habit of always picking up the check is becoming a problem. I don't see how we'll be able to afford it. The look on his face when he's able to treat friends and family to dinners, theater, vacations — it would break his heart to have to stop. I don't want to ask him to spend the rest of our lives not doing what he loves most. Is there something we can do?"

There are lots of conflicts around money, some that are out in the open, others that are unspoken. Help your couples have an open, honest discussion. They're looking to you for advice, but also to provide a safe place to have an open dialogue. You don't have to solve their differences, simply bring them to light. Then, send them off for further discussion among themselves.

ACTION STEPS:

* A great question to ask both parties is, "What are your concerns about money and the future?"
* Follow up with, "Is there anything you're doing now that you think needs to change?"
* Also ask each person, "What are your financial responsibilities?" Even spouses who don't work have financial responsibilities.
* Ask about their concerns. Ask about their visions. When they realize their visions are not in synch, send them off for further discussion.

Selling to Couples Tip #3 — Respect different decision making styles

In our chapter on the differences between men and women we learned that men tend to process quickly, while women tend to process completely. He has a desire to take action while she has a desire to think it through.

It's important to make sure the wife doesn't feel rushed, and the husband doesn't feel like you're getting off track.

ACTION STEPS:

For men:
* Always have an agenda for the meeting, and clearly state the action you want to accomplish by the end of the meeting.
* Find ways to tie discussions to his stated goals. You can do this by laying out each step of the process. "In Step One — we'll talk

about your visions of the future. In Step Two — we'll get into details of your specific financial situation. In Step Three — we'll talk about investment strategy and how we're going to reach your financial goals."

For women:

✳ If you have a list of questions you'll be asking, send that list to her ahead of time so she can prepare. She will appreciate the chance to think through her answers ahead of time. The more processing she does ahead of time, the less processing she needs to do in your office.

✳ Be prepared to share more information if she wants it, and take extra time to answer all her questions and concerns.

✳ Have supporting material: brochures, DVD's, comparison charts and answers to FAQ's (Frequently Asked Questions) that she can take home and look over later.

Selling to Couples Tip #4 — Understand different investment timelines

In our chapter on the differences between men and women we looked at men's focus on immediate gain vs. women's focus on long-term benefits.

He may be looking for financial products or decisions that pay off sooner rather than way down the road. He wants to be able to measure his progress quarterly, weekly, even daily. As a result, he may want to make more changes to try to take advantage of short-term opportunities.

She may be willing to give up some short-term upside if she can get guarantees of longer-term payoffs. Her "let it ride" approach can be a good thing. But a mistake women can make is holding on to something for too long. There may be a stock she's held for a long time, and it's a good time to sell, but she won't because she's emotionally attached to it. (This can happen to men as well.)

Be ready to accommodate both styles. There are times when staying the course is the wisest decision and times when it's necessary to make adjustments to take advantage of new opportunities.

ACTION STEPS:

For Men:

✳ Look at the whole portfolio and talk about the parts of the portfolio designed specifically for asset growth. THEN look at products designed to protect those gains. And phrase it in that exact manner "protecting gains" rather than "protecting against market downturns."

✳ If there is an immediate benefit, let him know. For example, when buying insurance, let him know how much cheaper it is if he buys now when he's healthy. Acting now will actually save him money down the road.

For Women:

✳ If she's emotionally attached to an investment and hanging on when she should be selling, tell her why now's a good time to sell, and let her know she can always buy back in at a later point.

✳ Be aware of her long time horizon. For example, be sure to address her fear that the insurance company may no longer be around or able to pay the claim 20 or 30 years down the road. She's thinking that far ahead.

Selling to Couples Tip #5 — Understand his *"That won't happen to me"* mindset

We looked at brain research that shows men focus on rewards, while women focus on rewards but also consequences. It's especially important to understand this dynamic when selling to couples.

He tends to think, "That's not going to happen to me," while she's thinking, "But what if that did happen?"

Let's look at a long-term care insurance example. Men and women tend to approach this product from different mindsets.

For men: When you're selling long-term care insurance to men, you're often met with resistance. In his mind, he is probably thinking, "That's not going to happen to me." He is focused on achieving his financial goals and doesn't want to spend money on something he's probably never going to use.

If he does accept that something might happen, his response is usually, "If something happens to me, my wife, daughters and family can take care of me." Or, "I'll just pay for it myself." Again, he may not have really thought through what an event would look like, what kind of care he would need or how much it would really cost. Let him know 75% of people 65 and older will eventually need long-term care.[1]

Spell it out for him with two contrasting stories of a husband who got long-term care insurance and one who didn't, and look at the different outcomes. Educate him on costs and what an actual event looks like. He probably has not painted that picture in his mind. Paint it for him.

"John purchased a long-term care policy. When he was diagnosed with Parkinson's disease, he was able to get the home care he needed so his wife didn't face the burden of his care alone. Instead of selling off assets, much of the cost was covered by their LTC policy. Stan, on the other hand, did not purchase a long-term care policy. The care fell mainly to his wife whose health declined so badly she could no longer care for him by herself and needed to bring in outside help. It cost nearly $70,000 a year for 7 years. That's almost a half a million dollars gone from their retirement fund that she was counting on to support herself and to someday pass along to the kids. Their kids lost their inheritance due to a long-term care event."

These are just a few of the ways to address his *"It won't happen to me"* challenges.

For women: Women also suffer from the *"It won't happen to me"* syndrome. But with their brain hard-wired to plan ahead and avoid bad outcomes, they may be more likely to sit down and really think through what an event would look like, who would provide the care and how much it could actually cost.

ACTION STEPS:

For men:

* Prepare for his *"That won't happen to me"* challenges. Share contrasting stories, and paint a vivid picture that helps him really think through what would happen.
* Stress how "protection" helps him maintain the gains from the other areas of his portfolio.

For women:

* Stress "protection" products that address her worst-case scenario worries.
* Be her ally. When he is stuck in *"That won't happen to me"* mode, shift the conversation to the wife's needs and concerns. Get him off *"That won't happen to me"* and onto *"How will this affect her?"* She will appreciate this.

Selling to Couples Tip #6 — Watch your body language

This could be a complete chapter in itself, but I want to give you one key piece of advice about body language. When a woman nods her head, she is not necessarily agreeing with you. Women nod their head to let you know they are engaged, listening and encouraging you to continue.

Male advisors — if she is nodding during a sales presentation, do not think she's on board with everything you're saying. She may simply want to let you know she is engaging with you. Be especially aware if she is nodding then stops. This is a sign there is a problem.

Female advisors — be aware of your head nodding as well, especially when you are selling to men. Here's a great story shared by a woman who attended one of my seminars:

"I was giving a sales presentation with my colleague, Ann. Ann has a habit of nodding her head in the affirmative when she is fielding questions or having a discussion. A lot of women do this unconsciously. It is our way of conveying the fact that we are listening and encouraging the person who is speaking. The problem is, many men mistake nodding for affirmation. If a woman nods, a man assumes she is agreeing with him.

After observing Ann, I pulled her aside and commented, 'You may be unaware of what you are communicating with your body language.'

Ann wasn't sure what I was referring to.

I said, 'When you nod your head, it comes across that you are agreeing with him. When I talk to men, I look them straight in the eye and strive to not move my head. You, as a woman, are more credible to a man with less head nodding and more direct body language.'"

This is an important point. I am also a nodder, which I realized when I saw myself on video and TV. I looked like a bobble head doll. When I speak to men or am on camera, I make a conscious effort to maintain eye contact and keep the nodding to a bare minimum, or not at all. Men feel like you're sending a mixed message when you nod but then later come back and disagree with them. It's also important for women to come across as calm and confident. When you nod too much you can appear too eager to please or emotional. So be aware of your body language and the message it sends.

For more tips on body language and how women can do a better job of selling to men, visit www.SellingFinancialServices ToWomen.com

ACTION STEPS:

＊ Don't mistake nodding for agreement. When a woman nods, she may simply be signaling she is engaged and listening to you.
＊ For women especially, be aware of your tendency to nod during conversations. When selling to men, keep the nodding to a minimum.

CONCLUSION:

When selling to couples, include both decision makers in the sales process. Ask questions to draw out each individual's goals and concerns. And understand how men and women approach financial decision making and financial products in a different way. This is especially important when selling insurance, which we'll look at in-depth next.

HOW TO SELL INSURANCE TO WOMEN

Remember the brain research where men and women were put into an MRI and played an investment game? In men's brains, the reward center lit up. In women, the reward center lit up, but so did the consequence center. With their long-term planning, consequence-avoiding brains, women are hard-wired to look for ways to protect themselves and the people they care about.

Can you say insurance anyone?

Insurance is a women's issue. It addresses women's three main concerns:

1. Leaving themselves and their family unprotected
2. Outliving their money
3. Being a burden on others

Life Insurance

It's long been established that if you're a guy, and you get married and have kids, you should get life insurance. Women, on the other hand, have not been expected to have as much life insurance as men, either because they are stay-at-home moms or not the primary breadwinner. But looking at the trends, we see more and more women are either contributing to or becoming the main breadwinner. Life insurance for her is the new must-have.

Current trends lead to three big opportunities for selling life insurance to women:

1. Making sure she has enough life insurance and the right kind of insurance.
2. Using life insurance as an inheritance vehicle to get money to her kids and grandkids or to organizations she cares about.
3. Partnering with her in the sales process to increase the amount of life insurance on her husband and to make sure they have the right type of insurance to meet their needs and lifestyle.

Make sure she has enough life insurance

While the numbers are getting better, women are still underinsured when it comes to life insurance.

Some women have a life insurance policy through work, but is it enough? And what happens if she leaves that job? In today's job market where employees regularly change companies and even careers, it's important to make sure women and men have a policy that will follow them wherever they go. Since many women go into and out of the workforce more often than men (taking time off to have children), this is especially important for them.

Using life insurance as an inheritance vehicle

Women in their 50's, 60's and 70's are looking for financial planning ideas to pass money to their kids and grandkids in a tax efficient manner. They want to give their children a leg up in life. Life insurance can be a great vehicle for that. Chances are if she has a husband, he will predecease her, so making children beneficiaries could be a smart move.

Women are also looking for ways to support causes they care about. Have a discussion with her about the difference she hopes to make in the world and the causes she supports.

Just a quick note about beneficiaries: Make sure you revisit this issue regularly in your reviews, especially in light of a death or divorce.

Include her in the sales process when selling life insurance to him

I've heard a lot of anecdotal evidence that when the woman is included in the life insurance sale, she will want a policy with a higher death benefit to make sure the family is properly covered. One advisor told me the story of a couple with four young kids. The husband wanted to purchase a $750,000 life insurance policy. Or, in his words, a policy that paid "Three quarters of a mil."

His wife turned to him and said, "If you die and that's all you leave us, I'm going to hunt you down, pull you out of the grave and kill you again." She wasn't satisfied until they had a two million dollar policy. I've heard many other similar stories.

While he may be looking for a number that sounds impressive, *three quarters of a mil*, she's really thinking through household expenses, paying the mortgage, paying for college and other costs of supporting her family.

ACTION STEPS:

✳ Review her life insurance. Make sure she has insurance, she has enough, and if her policy is through work, discuss a separate policy that could follow her throughout her career.

✳ For women in their 50's, 60's and even older, discuss using life insurance as an inheritance vehicle for efficient wealth transfer.

✳ When you're selling life insurance to him, make sure she is in the room and happy with the amount of life insurance he's carrying. Include both of them in the discussion so the husband can hear the logic for the amount she wants for the life insurance policy.

Annuities

Smart Money magazine did a piece in their October 2010 issue called "Why Women Get a Raw Deal in Retirement."[1] On average, women have less money in their retirement accounts. They also tend to live longer than men. These are just a few of the problems women face in funding and protecting their retirement. But there are things women can do to help themselves.

The article points to two products that fit perfectly with women's retirement needs: annuities and long-term care insurance.

The two biggest threats to a woman's retirement are:

1. She outlives her money
2. She has a major health event

These products address those threats. Yet many advisors aren't recommending them, especially annuities. Why? Part of the problem is that when men take the lead in investment discussions, they can be more short-term and present oriented. They're focused on returns versus the benefits specific to annuities.

Annuities address one of women's biggest financial fears, outliving their money. By taking a portion of their portfolio and putting it into an annuity, women can have guaranteed income for life. Depending on the amount, they can have some or most of their monthly expenses paid for by an annuity. Since women are living longer, this is a huge benefit.

Look at your female clients and ask them about their financial fears. If outliving their money is one of them, discuss the income for life feature of an annuity. Perhaps they have a big chunk of money in a CD. An annuity might be a better use for that money.

If the plan is to live off her husband's pension or social security, what happens when he's gone? An annuity can help provide the monthly income she needs to survive.

It's true that some clients are afraid of annuities because they don't understand them, yet so many are looking for the exact benefits an annuity can provide.

Consider these stats:

- 56% of pre-retirees and retirees do not expect to receive enough income from Social Security and employer pensions to cover their basic living expenses in retirement.
- 44% of these individuals express interest in converting a portion of their savings into guaranteed income in order to fill the gap between their retirement income and expenses.[2]

So have conversations with your clients about guaranteed income for life. It's a conversation they want to have!

One final reason to talk to women about annuities is because of their desire not to be a burden on their families. In a survey of non-qualified annuity owners, 81 percent said they will use their annuity savings to avoid being a financial burden on their children.[3]

ACTION STEPS:

- ✳ Discuss her financial fears. If she is afraid of outliving her money, introduce the guaranteed income for life option of an annuity.
- ✳ If she has money in a CD, consider moving it to an annuity where her money will work harder for her.
- ✳ Talk to her about how she can use the income from an annuity to help support herself so she won't be a financial burden to her children.
- ✳ You don't have to be an annuity expert. Just start the conversation. Many advisors have insurance experts they can bring in to do the heavy lifting. But you'll be the hero for providing a solution to her biggest fear.

Long-term care insurance

The *Smart Money* magazine article also mentioned the importance of long-term care insurance for women's retirement portfolios. I firmly believe every woman in America should have long-term care insurance. Remember, the two biggest threats to a woman's retirement portfolio are living too long, and the expense of a long-term health event. The cost of health care is only going up. Long-term care insurance is a no-brainer for smart women and for smart men as well.

So why don't more women and men have long-term care insurance? A part of the problem is the fact that the public still isn't exactly sure what long-term care insurance is and what it covers.

People still think it's nursing home insurance
There's still a perception among the public that long-term care insurance is strictly for nursing home care. But most of the insurance carriers I work with say the majority of their long-term care insurance claims are for in-home care. Harley Gordon is an elder law attorney and creator of the Certified in Long-term Care (CLTC) program www.ltc-cltc.com. He preaches that, "Long-term care insurance isn't nursing home insurance; it's staying out of nursing home insurance." Long-term care insurance can allow your clients to choose the kind of care they want, who gives that care and where that care is given.

People think Medicare and Medicaid will cover everything
Another problem is that many people have misperceptions about what coverage Medicare and Medicaid provide. This is why it's so important to bring up this subject with your clients and have an educational conversation. (Or bring in a Medicare/Medicaid expert to do a seminar for your clients.)

People don't know how much a long-term care event costs

A third problem is the lack of education about how much a long-term care health event can cost.

I gave a presentation a few years ago where I met an insurance agent who shared her "Two Million Dollar Woman" story. Her mother had a stroke in her early 70's and needed to be put into a nursing home. She still needs full-time care, but is not showing signs of any other problems. The agent's mother has now been in a nursing home for over 15 years at a cost of nearly two million dollars.

Another challenge many families face is dealing with a loved one with dementia. Ten years is now the average time a person is expected to live after being diagnosed with Alzheimer's disease.[4]

That's a lot of years of specialized care that can add up to a large amount of money.

Have these conversations with your clients. Remember, 75% of people 65 and older will eventually need long-term care.[5]

There is a high likelihood your client will face a long-term care event. Make sure they are protected with long-term care insurance.

Selling long-term care to couples

Margie Barrie is an expert in long-term care insurance. She is the National Marketing Coordinator of LTCP Designation, an LTC columnist for *Senior Market Advisor* magazine and Vice President of the 3 in 4 Need More Association. Margie has some valuable tips to help you be more successful when selling long-term care insurance.

Women are a very important part of the long-term care insurance sales process and appointment, particularly when working with married couples.

Many times the only reason that the agent has an appointment with a couple is because the wife has insisted on that meeting. And, frequently, women are the decision makers in this sale.

Here are several tips to assist you when working with female prospects:

1. During the face-to-face appointment, focus on the female. Observe her body language and make sure her questions are answered thoroughly and promptly. You need to establish a trusting relationship with her.

2. When talking about caregiving, emphasize that this is a women's issue. Explain how hard it is to be a caregiver.

Use facts like these:

- Today's women are going to spend more years taking care of their aging parents than they spent raising their own children.
- Caregivers are three times more likely to get sick, and that risk does not go down when the person they are taking care of dies.
- More caregivers are women — 61% vs. men 39%

3. When teaching an agent workshop, I do this exercise:

Select two agents from the audience, preferably a large male and a petite female.

Sit them in side by side chairs.

Explain to the class that they are married.

Describe the scenario: They are sitting in the family room, watching television. I hand the husband the remote for the slides and tell him it is a TV remote. The husband has had a stroke. He is still able to stay home, but needs help transferring, etc.

The husband has to go the bathroom. What do you do?

I then ask the female, "How many times do you think you will be able to help carry your husband to the bathroom?"

The female ALWAYS replies, "Maybe once, if I'm lucky, but no more than that."

Then reverse the situation. The wife has had the stroke (let the husband keep the TV remote.) Then ask the wife if her husband would be a good caregiver.

I then share a personal story about when I had major dental surgery. The oral surgeon told my husband to give me a pain pill when we got home so I could "stay ahead of the pain." My husband did so, and then woke me up every three hours to give me another pain pill. The problem was, he forgot to give me food. After taking three strong pain pills, plus the valium that the oral surgeon told to me to take that morning, I got up in the middle of the night to go to the bathroom and promptly fainted.

I conclude the scenario with, "Would I want my husband to be my caregiver? His heart is in the right place, but I don't think so."

When I finish that story, you can see the heads of the women in the audience nodding in agreement.

4. Don't be surprised if the woman refuses to make a decision to buy at the first appointment or refuses to let her husband make the buying decision. Sometimes, women need time to process their decisions. I am a firm believer in the two-call close. (If you can close the sale in one visit, fine, but don't be disappointed if you cannot.) I do try to close the sale two to three times in my first appointment, but if I can't, I use this script: "Here's what I would like to do: I have provided you with a lot of information about this protection, and I have even more information to leave with you. Let's set our next appointment in one week. That gives you enough time to review all the information, but you will not have forgotten it by then. So, does next Tuesday evening or Wednesday afternoon work better for you?"

Margie Barrie knows how to make long-term care real for people. Take Margie's advice and paint a vivid picture for your clients.

The "Use someone else's money" argument

Wendy Boglioli is a Gold Medal Olympic swimmer. Her athletic talents are equaled by her passion for long-term care insurance. Wendy has been a Long-Term Care Planning Specialist for over 14 years and is a National Spokesperson for Genworth Financial.

Wendy often tells the story of a very wealthy client who purchased long-term care insurance. The client had plenty of money to pay for her own care, but she made a business decision to buy long-term care insurance instead. The client's rationale was, "I built my business leveraging other people's money. If I can give you a check for a few thousand dollars a year and not use my money to pay for care, that's a smart business decision."

Men and women want to make smart business decisions. Wendy took this financial lesson to heart and bought her own long-term care insurance policy at age 42.

This brings up an important point. One of the best ways to convince clients of the importance of long-term care insurance is to show them that you have a policy yourself.

Men don't want to feel vulnerable

One more point about selling long-term care insurance to couples. Men do not like to talk about a situation where they picture themselves in a weakened state, having to rely on others for care. They do not want to think of themselves as vulnerable. So instead of hitting his vulnerable button, hit his provider/protector button. Frame long-term care insurance for him as something he does for his wife. The cost of his care will deplete assets, and if he dies first, will leave her alone with less money. Men do not want to leave their wives alone and destitute after they are gone.

ACTION STEPS:

For men:

✷ Stress how taking action now can save him immediate money. By purchasing a policy when he is younger and healthier, he can get it more cheaply. And policies for couples are usually less expensive than a policy for one or the other.

✷ Educate him about the underwriting process. By the time many clients realize they need long-term care insurance, they may not be insurable if they have had an event or their health has declined.

✷ A long-term care event can destroy a couple's portfolio. Educate him on just how much it costs. Visit www.genworth.com to use the Genworth Financial Cost of Care Calculator to view cost of care in your state.[6]

✷ When he says he will "pay for it himself," aka self insure, ask him which asset he would sell first. Make it real for him.

✷ Talk about how he can make a smart business decision and use someone else's money (the insurance company's money) to pay for care.

✷ Instead of hitting his vulnerable button, hit his provider/ protector button. Stress that getting a policy on him is actually something he should do for his wife, so the cost of his care won't leave her vulnerable financially.

✷ If he simply believes he will never need it, look at link benefit products that include some long-term care protection as part of a life insurance or annuity product.

✷ Talk to him about getting policies on his and his wife's aging parents. Want to get his attention? Ask him what would happen if one of their parents had to come live with them. What would that look like? What effect would that have on his relationship with his wife? Marriages across the country are strained and even broken by this situation.

For women:

✷ Discuss who will provide care. She is usually outliving her husband and may not have someone readily available to provide onsite care.

✳ Stress that long-term care insurance gives her control over who delivers the care and where that care is delivered. She wants control over where and how care is provided. She doesn't want to end up on Medicaid in a nursing home far from those she loves.

✳ Talk through possible care scenarios. Since women are the caretakers, they understand the cost, both personal and financial, of providing full-time care. This issue is very real for them.

✳ Discuss how long-term care events can hurt family relationships. She doesn't want to be a burden to family members. This is huge. A long-term care event can tear families apart in so many ways.

A friend of mine from New York took two years out of her life to move to New Jersey to care for her mother who had Alzheimer's disease. Her brother did nothing. But since she was not married at the time, she made the move to provide this end-of-life care for her mother.

After her mother died, my friend and her brother discovered their mother split everything 50/50 between them in her will. My friend felt this was not fair. She wanted to be compensated for the two years of her life she devoted to caring for her mother. Her brother said, "That was your choice," and refused to compensate her. They are now in a lawsuit and barely speaking.

Share these stories with your clients. These are real-life examples of the tensions and destruction caused by long-term care events.

CONCLUSION:

These insurance examples illustrate how insurance addresses women's key concerns. When you're selling insurance, make sure women are in the room and part of the decision making process. Insurance is a women's issue. She can be your best ally in the sales process. Next we'll look at another way women can be your biggest ally with the power of their recommendations and referrals.

9

REFERRALS — HOW TO GENERATE WORD OF MOUTH

Because of their more deliberate decision making process, women may take longer to decide to work with you or buy from you. But because they've put in the time and effort to check you out, they tend to have more confidence in your recommendations.

Once you've passed their test, women can be extremely loyal. If they have a good experience with you and trust you, they want to tell their network about you. Remember, a lot of women have had bad experiences with the financial industry. They and their friends are actively looking for someone they can feel good about doing business with. If she decides you are that person, you have a huge opportunity to get new business from her trusted network.

Women constantly share referrals

Ask any woman where she found her pediatrician, accountant, favorite coffee shop, hairdresser, real estate agent and yes, financial advisor, and she'll likely tell you, "A friend recommended him/her/it."

While men often turn to subject experts for opinions, women turn to other women like themselves. Women build relationships by sharing information. They share their experiences and opinions about products and professionals. If they have a good experience, they want to share this knowledge to help out their family and friends. That's why women refer so often. They're having these conversations all the time.

I was reminded of this when I went to a friend's house and remarked on her beautiful patio. Her husband said, "Yeah, we just had it redone."

My friend, his wife, said, "The carpenter did such a great job. He does all sorts of work around the house. He's really terrific. Here's his card with his information. Call him if you need someone who's reliable and affordable."

Women refer more than men, making them valuable customers

Here are a few insights from Tony Fannin, CEO of BE Branded and TJ Couzens, President of Brand X Research, the research arm of BE Branded, dedicated to understanding the women's market.

A man will refer his financial institution to 2.6 people on average. A woman, if treated well, will refer you to 21 of her friends. This is huge and is worth billions of dollars over the long-term.[1]

In the area of retention, men change brokers about every three years, while women, if treated well, stay with their advisors for 10+ years.[2] One of the reasons for this is men like bragging rights for great stock performance, so they will jump around if their portfolio is lagging behind their buddies. This leads to high client turnover for financial professionals. Women, on the other hand, invest based on their relationship with their advisor. If the advisor earns her trust and confidence, she will seek his or her advice and stay loyal because the relationship is valued more than bragging rights. Women may be harder to convince, but once convinced, they are more loyal in the long haul.

This is why it's so important to take the time to build relationships with your female clients and customers. Once you've put in the work to build their trust, women refer more than men, and they are more loyal. It's a total win-win. Women drive in more new business, and help you retain the business you already have.

To ask or not to ask, that is the question

Should you ask for referrals? Or will that turn off your clients? I've talked with financial professionals who have had great success asking directly for referrals, and others who believe the best way is to generate rather than ask for referrals. (More on generating referrals in just a minute.)

It is acceptable to ask for referrals, but it has to be the right time and place.

Here's an example of the wrong way to ask for referrals. You've just concluded a piece of business — let's say your client has just written you a check for a life insurance policy. Now you plop down a piece of paper with five lines on it and ask your client to write down the names of five friends who might be interested in life insurance.

Your client has just given something to you (a check and their business). Asking for more at that point feels unfair. And it puts your client in an uncomfortable position if they have to start writing down names while you're standing over them. They feel pressured, and that is not good.

When to ask for a referral

Some professionals do ask and have generated a lot of business by asking directly for referrals. If you do ask directly for referrals, do it at a time where there is no selling going on.

For example, if you're calling to remind a client about a lunch-and-learn event at your office, remind her she can bring a friend who could benefit from your expertise. Be up front. Tell her you're always looking for an opportunity to educate and possibly work with female clients like herself.

This way you aren't putting your client on the spot. You're not asking her to fill out a card, but you've planted a seed in her head that you are looking to work with other clients like herself.

How to ask for a referral — Two key questions

You are in a meeting where you are not doing any selling. Let's say you are in an annual review meeting. Ask your clients two questions:

1. If there was one thing I could change about how we work together that would improve our relationship, what would it be?
2. What do you like best about working together?

The first question is designed to give your client permission to be open about anything he or she may not like. This is especially important for women who can be people pleasers and may not want to share anything negative.

The second question is designed to bring out what the client loves most about working with you. Take notes about what she says and ask her if you can share her thoughts with prospective new clients. This is the perfect opening to ask for referrals.

"I really enjoy working with clients like you. That's why I've built my business on referrals. My best new clients come from recommendations from my current clients. If you know of someone like you who's looking for financial guidance, please let me know."

If they have someone in mind, you can follow up with this question:

"What would be the best way to introduce myself to (referral name)?"

You are now putting her in control of how the introduction will take place. She knows this person and can recommend the best possible approach. She will also offer to introduce you herself.

Let her know what you'll do with her friend's contact information

If you do ask for contact information, be very clear about exactly how that information will be used.

Remember, she is the gatekeeper of her relationships. She's not going to just pass around her trusted network's information. If her friend has a bad experience, it could harm their relationship. And she is all about protecting her relationships and alliances.

So if you ask for information, be clear about how you'll use it. "I'll contact Betty by email to see if there's interest in working together. I'll follow up with one phone call. That's it. If there isn't mutual interest, I won't contact her again."

Share something about your current client and why you enjoy working with her

One advisor shared a technique he uses to great advantage. If a client has someone they would like to refer, he gets the contact information and makes the first contact. In that contact he points out something specific he likes about his current client. For example, "(Prospective client), Terry Smith gave me your name. Terry has been a client of mine for over 10 years. What I love most about Terry is her ability to make people feel special. At our annual client appreciation events, she makes a point to find people who may not know anyone and makes introductions and brings them into conversations. I just love that about her. She is a delight to work with."

Well, of course the prospective client shares the advisor's compliment with Terry. This advisor says he almost always hears from the current client thanking him for saying something so nice about her. This not only provides a wonderful introduction to a referral, but it also strengthens the relationship between the advisor and his existing clients.

Generate referrals — Give her something to talk about

Women have discussions every day about the people they work with. Are your clients talking about you? Are you giving them a reason to talk about you (a good reason)?

When I first met Ron Seilback (who wrote the preface), we met for breakfast before an event at which I was speaking. Ron walked up, introduced himself and gave me a bag of Swedish Fish. For those of you who don't know what Swedish Fish are, they are red gummy candies in the shape of fish. I am addicted. It's a problem. I'm getting professional help.

Here's why Ron impressed me so much with this simple gesture. This wasn't a generic gift. A scented candle wouldn't have cut it. I wrote about my addiction to Swedish Fish in my book *The Soccer Mom Myth, Today's Female Consumer: Who She Really Is, Why She Really Buys*. The message Ron sent me by showing up with a bag of fish was, "I read your book, I paid attention and I remember what you wrote about." At that point, anything Ron wanted, he was going to get. He had me at, "Hello, I have Swedish Fish."

I tell this story everywhere I go. Ron was smart. He gave me something to talk about.

When you go above and beyond your normal responsibility, women notice AND they talk about it with their friends.

Here's another example. After my father passed away, my mother wanted to get an appraisal of his stamp collection. This came up during a conversation with her financial advisor. To his huge credit, the advisor hunted down a reputable appraiser and gave the information to my mother. He didn't want her to be taken advantage of by an appraiser that wasn't honest. This meant a lot to my mother, and she shared this story several times.

I met a very successful financial advisor in South Dakota. When I asked what made him so successful, he shared this story. One of his clients was diagnosed with cancer. He became very close to the family, making sure all of his client's financial affairs were in order, but also forming personal connections with the family members. At the funeral, the family invited him to sit in the family's private area rather than with the rest of the attendees. Many people asked who he was and were surprised to find out he was the family's financial advisor. They wanted his name since they couldn't imagine their FA providing that kind of time, energy and support. People looked at this advisor and saw the kind of caring, involved guy they wanted to work with.

Use email correspondence to generate referrals.
My financial advisor Peter Walls is brilliant in so many ways. He sends out regular emails with strategy and portfolio updates. He has client appreciation and educational events. And he ends most emails with this line, "If you know of someone who isn't getting this kind of personal attention from their financial advisor, please pass along my name."

I love this for two reasons. One, he is reinforcing that his current clients are getting personal attention and lots of communication. And two, he is asking, subtly, for referrals. One of my favorite emails came from Peter right before the Super Bowl. There was a huge snow storm in Richmond and the market was tanking. Peter sent out an email saying, "I just want you to know, most people are gone, but I'm still in the office and I'm on top of the market situation. If you have any questions or concerns, please call me." And, of course, he finished with, "If you're talking to someone at your Super Bowl party who isn't getting this kind of personal attention from their financial advisor, please pass along my name."

Brilliant.

Define who your ideal client is

Tell me if you notice a difference in these two phrases: "Do you know someone who could benefit from the guidance of a financial advisor?" "Do you know of any nurses who are single mothers who could benefit from the guidance of a financial advisor?"

I met a planner who had a previous history in health care. She loves working with nurses (male and female), doctors and other health care professionals. She knows nurses are networked like crazy, and many are single moms. So she tells her nurse clients that she specializes in working with nurses and also works with a lot of single moms. She gets referrals like crazy because she is so specific, and she has tapped into such a networked group. She is a single mom herself and so has instant credibility with this group.

So get specific when you ask for a referral. Who is your ideal client? Who do you want to work with? Special needs families? Women who are recently divorced or widowed? Pharmacists? Teachers? Women business owners? C-level executives? Let people know who your ideal client is and how you can help that person. Take for example the advisor I met who works with special needs families. He has a son who is autistic, so he understands personally the costs and financial needs associated with the care of his son. Word has spread in this community, and he just sits back and lets the referrals come to him.

Share why you want referrals

When you talk about your ideal client, let people know who that person is, and also, how you can help that person. Ask yourself these questions:

- Do you have a lot of experience or expertise in a specific area?
- Is there a specific way you make a real difference in people's lives?
- Why did you get into this business? Do you have a personal story of an event that had a significant impact on you?

Share who you want to help, how you can help them and why you want to help them.

The power of your personal story

Jean Carpenter-Backus is a Certified Public Accountant, Certified Financial Planner and a principal of Carpenter & Langford, PC, a CPA firm recognized by the *Austin Business Journal* as one of the top accounting firms in Austin, Texas. She has one of the most amazing personal stories I've heard. This is an incredibly successful woman with a very humble beginning.

At the tender age of 14, Jean was smitten with a boy who lied about his age to join the Army. They married, and when her high school biology teacher told her to "please shut up," she gathered her books, walked out and didn't look back. She moved with her husband to Germany. Their baby was born with a chromosomal disorder, and the marriage became abusive. She ran to the military police station when her husband pulled a gun on her and caught a plane back to America with her baby boy and the clothes on her back.

"I didn't quite know where I was going," she remembers.

The plane was bound for Washington, D.C. Fellow passengers took her and the baby to Walter Reed Army Medical Center because the infant needed surgery.

As she sat all alone and penniless in a deserted hospital corridor, an Army officer came and sat beside her. "You've got a hole in your shoe," he said, pointing to her black Mary Janes. "Let me take you to the post exchange and buy you a pair of shoes."

Jean was mortified, but finally relented. She asked how to repay the favor, but the officer told her to just "pass it on." Her introduction to the philosophy of pay-it-forward has stuck with her for 40 years.

Financial professionals have different levels of comfort about how much personal information they want to share. Choose how much you want to share and with whom you want to share it. But remember, men and women love a good story, especially when it involves overcoming adversity. Clients don't just want to work with a number cruncher; they want to work with a human being.

Ask for introductions

Are there specific people you want to get in front of? Are there successful influential people you'd love to have as clients or referral sources? Ask to meet them. Find someone who can make an introduction, or approach them yourself.

That's exactly what Cella Quinn did when she was building her financial advisor business. She approached 32 highly successful business women in her area and invited them to a special dinner at her country club. She let them know who else she invited and billed it as an exclusive gathering of like-minded, successful women who should know each other. She made it clear it was all about socializing and forming connections, and there would be no sales pitch involved. Thirty of 32 accepted. "I had actually expected all 32 to attend, so it was a bit disappointing," she quipped.

The night was a huge success, and many connections were made. The women enjoyed the event so much, they wanted to continue it on a regular basis, and so "The 10 Club" was born. (They meet on the 10th of every month.) By making it small, exclusive and fun, Cella was able to gather the high profile women she wanted to connect with. She also knew the women would want to meet others on her powerful guest list.

Take your cue from Cella Quinn. Is there a select group you'd like to meet? Create an exclusive gathering and invite them. Be transparent that these are simply people you feel should know each other. Almost everyone is looking to grow their network and is flattered to be invited. Invite people in non-competing areas. You may be pleasantly surprised by who shows up.

Guys, if you're thinking this only works for women, think again. Ask some of your high profile female clients if there are other professional women they'd like to meet and get to know. Offer to host an event and make the invitations. You will get HUGE credit for taking an interest. And there are advantages to being the only guy in the room. You are extremely memorable.

Educational seminars and client appreciation events

Almost all of the most successful financial professionals I talk with say their best sources of new clients and referrals are their educational seminars and client events. Whether it's getting up in front of a group of highly qualified prospects to share your knowledge or a "bring a friend" event where your clients bring someone they know to an event you sponsor, financial professionals tell me these are their highest converting prospecting activities.

Women especially love to attend seminars and events with their friends. So consider some women-only events where you can tap into the networks of your best female clients.

I also know male financial professionals who include their wives in these events, since many women bond with the wife as well as the male financial professional.

Remember the story of the advisor I talked with who hosted a retirement lunch for a female client who was retiring from her firm after 35 years. He invited her and ten of her friends to a retirement lunch celebration. Her friends were amazed that her advisor would do this for her. Even though no business was discussed during lunch, the focus was on the woman who was retiring, several of the women asked for the advisor's card, and he walked away with business.

Everyone wants to get in front of affluent women. Annette Bau is the founder of Advisor Marketing Practices, a CFP™ practitioner and has been a financial planner for more than 22 years. For the last five years, she has consulted and worked with advisors to help them tap into the affluent market niche including the affluent women niche. Annette shares some of her secrets for getting noticed by affluent women.

Referral Strategies that Guarantee Success

Two of the best strategies for generating referrals from affluent women are feeder workshops and relationship marketing.

Feeder Workshops

One of the most important skills you need to develop in becoming a top producer is to leverage your time. Speaking to different groups is one of the easiest strategies to leverage your time and increase your referrals.

I built my financial planning career speaking to groups, many that were comprised largely of women. In one of the community feeder workshops that provided continuing educational credit, a woman who had a net worth that exceeded 20 million dollars attended. She became my client and referred me to four other affluent women who also became my clients.

The secret to workshops is to interview members of the specific women's niche market you want to serve and then determine the topics that will be of most interest to them. You can find out more at www.FeederWorkshopSuccess.com/sell.

Relationship Marketing

Another successful strategy I use to generate referrals is relationship marketing. It is common for me to send out 100 heart-felt cards in a day. Samples of the best heart-felt cards for women include a Valentine's Day card with truffles, St Patrick's Day, Easter, Memorial Day, Mother's Day, July 4th, Thanksgiving, Holidays, their birthday and the day they became a client. These cards include photos and a handwritten note or inspirational quote. We then send out four referral cards, one each quarter. These include messages like, "Thanks for the referrals, We love referrals, We are looking for clients just like you and Who do you know?" While I have gotten numerous referrals from this strategy, more importantly, it has converted customers to clients for life.

Cultivating relationships is one of the most important aspects for generating business and acquiring more affluent women as clients. I acquired two of my largest eight-figure net worth clients as a result of relationship marketing. The key is to be relevant, create a relationship, educate, don't sell and bring value. The result in both cases was, when the time was right, they called me (one took 7 years and another 10 years).

I now have hundreds of advisors who use relationship marketing and who have also had amazing results. The secret is to automate the communication process so it happens whether you have time or not. Learn more at www.MillionDollarRelationshipMarketingSystem.com/sell.

Thanks Annette. I'll go more in depth on events and client communication in Chapter 11 — Marketing Financial Services to Women.

ACTION STEPS:

✳ Ask for referrals in a follow up meeting where no actual sale is taking place. Beware of asking her for names on the spot. High pressure referral solicitations turn off women.

✳ Ask the two questions designed to generate a conversation about testimonials and referrals.

✳ If you ask for her friend's contact information, ask her to make the introduction first. Also tell her exactly what you'll do with that contact information.

✳ In your introductory contact with the prospect, share something you like about your client who gave you the referral.

✳ Give her something to talk about. Go above and beyond your job and exceed her expectations.

✳ Define your ideal client. Let your clients know which niches you serve and why you want to work with them.

* Let clients know how you can help people and why you got into the business. Give them a story they can share.
* Ask for introductions. Just like Cella Quinn, come up with a list of people you'd like to meet and either find people in your network who can introduce you, or approach them directly for a gathering of like-minded professionals.
* Schedule educational events and "bring a friend" client appreciation events to get in front of new, qualified prospects. Use the events as a chance to share your knowledge and expertise, as well as to get to know prospective clients on a more personal level. Consider women-only events to tap into your most influential female clients.

CONCLUSION:

When you do a good job with women, they notice. Women can be a tremendous source of referrals. Educate them, celebrate their achievements, remember details about them and remind them of who your ideal client is (in many cases, women just like them). Though be aware, not all women are alike.

Up next, we'll meet four different types of women you'll likely work with in your practice. We'll look at their decision making processes and investment styles. We'll get specific about what you can do and questions you can ask to make sure you deliver the results each one is looking for.

10

THE FOUR TYPES OF FEMALE CUSTOMERS

One of the biggest mistakes financial professionals make is thinking women, as a mass, all think alike. I'm sure from your own personal experience you know that's not true. Women are incredibly varied in their decision making styles, values, needs and investment philosophies. You've probably run into many professional women who take charge of their whole financial situation, while other women rely heavily on the opinions of others. You've seen some women take big risks, while others are nearly paralyzed with fear.

In my research, I've run across many types of female investors, but I've narrowed it down to four to give you a framework to work within. Financial professionals I work with instantly recognize these four women.

So let's look at the four types, and I'll give you specific suggestions for how to deal with and connect with each type of female investor.

FOUR TYPES OF FEMALE INVESTORS

Traditional Tess	**Power Broker Pam**
Wants to feel safe	Wants to feel smart
Relationship Rosa	**Deliberate Debbie**
Wants to feel she can trust you	Wants to feel prepared

Overview of the four types

Traditional Tess
Tess could be a widow or married. If she is married, her husband is making the majority of the financial decisions. She has abdicated responsibility for money to someone else. She may not want to be included in meetings for fear the advisor will purposefully talk over her head. But she knows deep down she needs to better understand what's going on with her money.
+ Least knowledgeable
+ Afraid to ask questions
+ "Make decisions for me" (but explain why)
+ Low risk tolerance
+ Wants to feel safe

Power Broker Pam
Pam is usually a Type A personality. She is likely to be successful in her career or may be a business owner. She could also be an on-the-go mother with a full plate of activities. She is knowledgeable about money but would like to learn more. She likes to be in control but doesn't have time to stay on top of all of her investment decisions.
+ Most knowledgeable
+ Asks direct questions
+ "I make my own decisions" (but don't have time to stay on top of everything)
+ Most risk tolerant
+ Wants to feel smart

Relationship Rosa
Rosa could be married or single. She is likely a mother and very involved with her family including children, parents and siblings. She may appear scattered or unorganized and sometimes seems to veer off track during conversations. She is very open to your guidance and would like to have a comprehensive plan in place.

- Somewhat knowledgeable
- Asks some questions
- "Make decisions with me"
- Some risk tolerance
- Wants to feel she can trust you

Deliberate Debbie

Debbie could be single or married. She is very organized and thorough. She is also skeptical. She will come in with lots of questions. She may be coming from a place of fear and wants to share her concerns with you.

- Somewhat knowledgeable
- Asks the most questions
- "Get my approval before you make a decision" (no surprises)
- Least risk tolerant
- Wants to feel prepared

Now that you've gotten an overview, let's take a more in-depth look at the four types of women investors.

Traditional Tess

- She has the lowest tolerance for risk.
- She is most comfortable with CD's, bonds and conservative investments.
- She believes in Social Security and Medicare.
- Her husband does or did most of the planning.
- She relies on family members for advice.
- She is very focused on not making a mistake.

Traditional Tess Challenges

- Getting her involved – she fears meetings will be judgmental or over her head.
- Overcoming her fear of risk.
- Overcoming her fear of change.
- Understanding her family influencers.

Traditional Tess Questions
- Where are you from?
- What keeps you up at night?
- Who do you trust to give you financial advice?
- What's the one thing you absolutely do not want to happen?
- Who are the most important people in your life?
- How do you feel about the decisions we made? Are you comfortable with them?

Traditional Tess Client Meeting
- Include her in the meeting!
- Let her know ahead of time what you'll be going over in the meeting. (Let her know you want to get to know her better, find out what keeps her up at night, answer any questions she may have.)
- Talk about how, statistically, she's likely to outlive her husband and go over the plan of what would happen then.
- Make contact with her adult children — introduce yourself.
- Offer to meet her at her house. (This is a great way to make her feel more comfortable and gives her a chance to "host" you and show you her home/world.)

Power Broker Pam
- She has the highest tolerance for risk.
- She is results focused.
- She is highly educated.
- She wants options and choices — she is not looking for you to just do it for her.
- She wants to be in control.
- She wants a plan and wants to understand the strategy behind it.
- She cares about your credentials (she's going to Google you.)

Power Broker Pam Challenges
- High expectations — she is a perfectionist.
- She needs to feel important.

- She can be short-term focused.
- She has trouble turning over control.
- She doesn't want you to "do it for her."
- She will challenge you — she wants to know "why?"

Power Broker Pam Questions
- What's your opinion?
- What are your short-term and long-term goals?
- How will we measure success?
- What kinds of opportunities are you looking for?
- How have you gathered the wealth you have?
- What's the smartest financial decision you've made?
- If we were to work together, and it's now 12 months later, looking back a year, what did I do for you?

Power Broker Pam Client Meeting
- Make her feel important.
- Discuss goals.
- Focus on opportunities/performance.
- Explain the overall theory/strategy/plan.
- Share educational resources (reports, books, seminars).
- Give her control — give her options and let her choose.
- State your credentials.
- Be brief.
- Have an agenda.
- Work with her other experts (CPA, lawyer, estate planner) to coordinate a plan.

Relationship Rosa
- It's all about her extended family — kids, grandkids, parents, in-laws.
- She has a neutral risk tolerance.
- She is very relationship oriented, she is the caregiver.
- She gathers opinions of others but relies on own guidance system.

- She is focused on doing the right thing.
- She doesn't want to be a burden.

Relationship Rosa Challenges
- She is slow to make a decision.
- She suffers from inaction due to fear of making a mistake.
- She is slow to trust recommendations.
- She shares a lot of stories — she seems to get off track (she does not give short direct answers.)
- She apologizes, is sensitive, takes everything personally.
- She won't tell you when something's wrong (she'll just leave.)

Relationship Rosa Questions
- What did you learn about money from your parents?
- Who is affected by your financial decisions?
- What was your best and worst experience with money?
- What do you want out of this relationship? What do you expect from me as an advisor?
- How do you feel about the decisions we made? Are you comfortable with them?
- If there's one thing I could change to improve our relationship, what would it be?
- Is there anything else?

Relationship Rosa Client Meeting
- Spend lots of time up front "getting to know you" and sharing stories (on both sides).
- Share pictures of your family.
- Ask her what she's reading.
- Ask about kids, grandkids, parents, siblings and pets (seriously, don't forget the pets).
- Smile.
- Smile some more.
- Go deep — share why you got into the business, how you hope to make a difference in the world.

- Ask her what she's passionate about, including causes she supports.
- Ask her *why* she does what she does (job, passion, motherhood, grandmotherhood) and be prepared when she asks the same question of you.
- Do NOT go into anything scripted. She will pick up on it right away, and it will feel inauthentic.
- Share experiences of people in similar situations to hers.

Deliberate Debbie

- She is extremely risk aware.
- She is methodical and detail oriented.
- She does not like change.
- She wants to know she's protected in case something bad happens.
- She's looking for guarantees.
- She makes decisions based on what's worked in the past.
- She doesn't know where to start — it feels overwhelming.
- She is slow to take action.

Deliberate Debbie Challenges

- She doesn't want to be pushed into anything.
- She asks a lot of questions.
- She is slow to make a decision.
- She has a lot of concerns/objections.
- She is focused on past mistakes/problems.
- She will blame you if something goes wrong.
- She worries over every change in market.

Deliberate Debbie Questions

- What's keeping you up at night?
- Do you have any concerns we didn't cover?
- Have I answered all your questions?
- What are your sources for financial information?
- What was your best and worst experience with your previous advisor?

- What's the one thing I could change that would improve how we work together?

Deliberate Debbie Client Meeting
- Start and end on time.
- Anything she can fill out ahead of time, send to her ahead of time.
- Let her know before the meeting what she needs to bring — tax returns, insurance policies, financial records, etc.
- Send the agenda for the meeting to her ahead of time.
- Do NOT try to downplay her concerns.
- Be prepared for lots of questions.
- Have charts, graphs, anything visual and tangible that helps explain what you're talking about.
- Give her information she can take home and go over in more detail.
- Avoid any words that sound judgmental.

ACTION STEPS:

* Traditional Tess — Have a relationship with her. *Make her feel safe.*
* Power Broker Pam — Have a comprehensive plan and theory. *Make her feel smart.*
* Relationship Rosa — Focus on people and stories. *Win her trust.*
* Deliberate Debbie — Educate her. Share her values. *Make her feel prepared.*

CONCLUSION

All women do not think alike. Look at your clients. See if you recognize any of these women. If you're not sure which investment style a client falls into, try to incorporate a little bit of what each type wants.

WARNING: Do NOT show these to your clients. Everyone thinks they are unique and people do not like being labeled. We are taking an honest, realistic and sometimes not very flattering look at these investors.

DO show these to other people in your office and get their help in identifying which clients might fit these profiles. See if they have personal stories about how they've been successful with these types of clients. Get their thoughts on how to provide the customer experience each type is longing for.

Now that you have a good idea of how to sell to women, how do you attract these women to your practice? How do you get the message out? How do you win the hearts and minds of female consumers? Let's take a look.

MARKETING FINANCIAL SERVICES TO WOMEN

In order to successfully sell to women, you must first attract those women to your business. In this chapter we'll discuss the most effective ways to advertise and promote your company and your services to women. The chapter has three parts:

Part I — Images
Part II — Copy
Part III — Marketing Channels

When I started studying the marketing to women field almost a decade ago, I was, frankly, surprised that I couldn't find more research on how men and women responded to financial services advertising. I have a lot of experience in online marketing where we test ads. We put up version A and version B and see which version performs the best. In my work with clients, I found that men and women responded to different copy, different images and clicked on different areas of websites. In other words, some content performed better with women, some content performed better with men.

So what I'm sharing with you here is the result of many years of general research into which advertising and design elements are most persuasive when marketing to women. I've also done my own research on what copy and images are most effective when marketing financial services to women.

For example, in many retirement ads, you see a silver-haired couple. She is in a subservient position, with her head on his shoulder, or leaning into him, or he is carrying her (usually on a beach) or he is a visionary looking into the distance while she stands adoringly behind him.

Because these images are so prominent, I assume they must be effective. And they are — for men. They hit men's "provider and protector" button. But do they work for women as well? Let's find out.

Part I — Images

In my Women and Finance Survey, I showed images from actual financial services ads to two groups of women, one over 50 and one under 50. I started with images of couples where the woman was in a subservient position (leaning her head on his shoulder, being carried by him, standing behind him as he gazes into the distance, etc.) Remember, these are images from actual advertisements. Here's how the women responded to the following question:

When you see images like these in financial services ads, how do they make you feel?

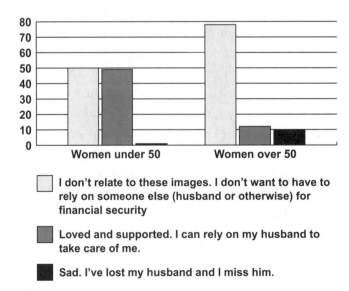

☐ I don't relate to these images. I don't want to have to rely on someone else (husband or otherwise) for financial security

▨ Loved and supported. I can rely on my husband to take care of me.

■ Sad. I've lost my husband and I miss him.

I found it really interesting that women under 50 didn't have as negative a reaction to the subservient couple images as the 50 plus group. Why did the women over 50 have such a negative reaction? Further research showed these women had several problems with the images.

1. They are divorced, and the husband who was supposed to take care of them is remarried with another family.
2. They've realized that they need to step up to the plate and take more responsibility for their finances. They are no longer simply relying on their husband to make all the decisions.
3. They have lost their husband, either to divorce or they are a widow, and they often are not remarrying.

Perhaps women under 50 are still in their first marriages. I don't have concrete answers. But the takeaway is — if you are targeting women of any age, be careful of images of couples where the woman is in a subservient position, especially with women over 50.

Which images did women respond to most favorably?

We tested other images from financial ads to see which ones got the most favorable response. Here are the images in order of preference:

1. Multi-generational family
2. Multi-generational group of three women
3. Professional woman
4. Couple but on an equal level

In both the under 50 and over 50 groups, the most favored images were the multi-generational group of three women and the family shots. This was especially effective when the people in the images were interacting.

To see the images from the research study, go to www.Selling FinancialServicesToWomen.com

A key benefit women want from money is to create a better life for their family. So put her family at the center of your marketing efforts.

Also, there really is truth to the idea that babies and puppies are irresistible. Use pictures of parents and grandparents interacting with kids. And include shots of people with their pets. Seriously. In my seminars I show images from financial ads with almost no emotional reaction. Then I show a great shot of a woman and her dog cuddling and it gets a big "Awwwwwwww," every time. According to an AP Petside.com poll, one out of three married women (33%) say their pets are better listeners than their husbands.[1]

So don't forget to include Fido in your financial services ads.

When you're deciding what images to include in your marketing materials, ask yourself what emotion you want those images to convey, for women and for men. Some images convey no emotion at all. Try to find unusual or interesting images that tell a story. A picture really is worth a thousand words.

ACTION STEPS

* If you're marketing to women over 50, use family shots or a group of women. Note, three or four seems to be the ideal number of people in an image.
* Show parents and grandparents interacting with kids.
* Include images of people, especially women with their pets.
* Include images that tell a story or break through stereotypes. (For example: a mother under the hood of a car explaining the parts to a son or daughter.)
* Put her and her family at the center of your marketing efforts and show her how you can help her create a better life for her family.

Part II — Copy

What copy is most persuasive with women? Why do so many women feel financial advertising is not speaking to them? Well, to be blunt, many financial services ads are written by men for men. There's a whole lot of male communication style going on. The focus is on status and achievement.

We provide wealth management services.

Our strategic advice and outstanding execution is informed by world-class insights and comprehensive access to the global capital markets.

We help our clients achieve their goals and highest aspirations.

Make your money work harder for you.

Make strategic decisions to maximize performance.

We open the right doors for our clients.

Profit from our powerful planning tools.

It's all about "wealth management" "taking control" "being the master of your destiny" and "achieving your dreams."

One financial website described long-term care insurance as "A firewall for your retirement plan." I'm just curious, how many 50 plus women (and men) relate to the firewall comparison (or know what a firewall is)?

From what we learned about male vs. female communication style, the above language may be missing the mark with women.

So in my Women and Finance Survey we asked women what money and financial security means to them. Here are some of their answers.

What financial issues are you most concerned about?

WOMEN UNDER 50	WOMEN OVER 50
1. Feeling financially secure	1. Feeling financially secure
2. Retirement planning	2. Having a comprehensive plan in place
3. Getting out of debt	3. Retirement planning
4. Having a comprehensive plan in place	4. Outliving my money
5. Outliving my money	5. Getting out of debt

WOMEN UNDER 50	WOMEN OVER 50
6. Socially responsible investing	6. Wealth management
7. Wealth management	7. Socially responsible investing

We can see with both groups that feeling financially secure is their top financial concern. Wealth management, which is what many companies tout as their main benefit, is last or next to last on their lists.

Having a comprehensive plan in place ranks fairly high with both groups (#4 with women under 50 and #2 with women over 50). We know from the research on women's brains that "comprehensive" is a benefit they are looking for with their holistic brain focus.

It's no surprise that "getting out of debt" is bigger with women under 50 who are probably carrying more debt. This could be important language for financial professionals targeting women under 50.

I want to share a quick note about "socially responsible investing." I think part of the problem is the verbiage. The vast majority of women care about charitable causes and giving back to their communities. In her book *Women Wealth and Giving, The Virtuous Legacy of the Boom Generation*, author Margaret May Damen has lots of information and research on the subject.[2]

I believe women want to put that money to direct use. Rather than being interested in "socially responsible investing" which may sound like "financial products" they may have a separate pile of money they want to give directly to the charities and organizations of their choice.

So don't take the low rank of "socially responsible investing" to mean women don't care about socially responsible causes. It may be that instead of finding a socially responsible mutual fund, you could help them set aside money in a "giving fund" with a set amount every year that they can donate directly to the causes of their choice.

What does having money allow you to do?

WOMEN UNDER 50	WOMEN OVER 50
1. Provide for your family	1. Take care of yourself and the people you love
2. Take care of yourself and the people you love	2. Not have to rely on others
3. Prepare for the future	3. Prepare for the future
4. Protect your family	4. Achieve financial independence
5. Plan for your future	5. Plan for your future
6. Not have to rely on others	6. Be responsible
7. Be responsible	7. Provide for your family
8. Achieve financial independence	8. Protect your family
9. Keep your promises	9. Keep your promises

There's a really interesting difference between women under 50 and women over 50. The women under 50 are focusing on previously male dominated roles like "providing for your family" (#1 women under 50, but #7 women over 50) and "protect your family" (#4 women under 50, #8 women over 50).

"Not having to rely on others" is fairly strong with both, but particularly strong (#2) with women over 50.

"Take care of yourself and the people you love" ranks high with both groups. Language around family and caretaking scores high with women.

Language including the word "prepare" also scores well with both groups.

Interestingly, "achieving financial independence" which is language you see everywhere is only #4 with women over 50 and #8 with women under 50. I believe a key reason is that the word "independence" can have a different meaning for women and men.

Independence vs. interdependence — A key difference between men and women

Men tend to see relationships as hierarchical. In order to be independent, they must be dominant rather than subordinate. For many men, being independent includes having someone dependent on them. This also taps into men's role as provider and protector. For men, independence signifies status and power.

For women, independence is about autonomy; it's about the ability not to be dependent on someone else. It's not a matter of being dominant or subordinate.

This can help explain why so many financial images show a man with a woman dependent upon him. This actually signals status and "independence" to men. But knowing that women view independence as *not* having to be dependent, we see how those images can backfire with women.

Be careful how you use the word "independence" and the images you associate with it since it may have different meanings for men and women.

"Being able to" vs. "Not having to" — Consequence avoidance vs. goal achievement

Another verbal trend I noticed in my Women and Finance Survey was women's focus on avoiding consequences vs. achieving goals.

In answer to the open question, "Having financial security means.....," many of the responses started with "not having to" vs. "being able to." "Not having to" is a consequence avoiding phrase. It focuses on what you do NOT want to happen. "Being able to" is a goal achievement phrase. It focuses on what you DO want to happen.

In the survey, there were some goal achievement answers like:
Having enough money to live comfortably
Being able to sleep soundly at night

But there were just as many consequence avoidance answers like:
Never having to worry about money again
No worries about where the money is going to come from when I need it
Not depending on anyone else
Not having to eat cat food as I age
Not worrying about money anymore and being able to help my children (which is a combination of both consequence avoidance and goal achievement)

Also remember that more women chose to read, "The four biggest mistakes in retirement planning and how to avoid them" vs. "The four secrets to having the retirement of your dreams."

I noticed on a recent visit to www.seniormarketadvisor.com that the number one most read article was "5 Lame Questions Advisors Need to Avoid." Both men and women can be motivated by language which focuses on avoiding consequences and bad outcomes. (By the way, be sure to read chapter 13 — The Client Meeting — Women-Winning Questions to see what questions you *should* be asking your clients.)

Look at your headlines and test to see if consequence avoiding headlines like "Worried about not having enough money in retirement?" will work better than achieving goal headlines like "Achieve financial independence." NOTE: If you have a consequence avoiding headline, always follow it up with positive goal achievement copy in the rest of the marketing piece.

For example: "Worried about not having enough money in retirement? At XYZ Financial Company, we believe the best way to prepare for tomorrow is to plan today. No matter what shape your finances are in, we can discuss your goals and concerns and create a comprehensive plan for the future. Financial security is within reach. It starts with a phone call. XYZ Financial Company. Our clients sleep at night."

Not wanting to run out of money is the consequence avoiding piece. Sleeping at night and achieving financial security are the goal achievement pieces. Experiment with different combinations to see what works best.

Part III — Marketing Channels

Which channels are most effective for reaching women? That's a question I'm asked quite often. The answer is — it depends on your budget. If you have the money, TV and radio are still effective channels for reaching women. Whether you have a big budget or no budget, I'm a huge fan of having an online presence. Women are spending more time online than almost anywhere else. But there are lots of ways to reach out and connect with women. In this chapter, we'll look at the following marketing channels:

1. Your website
2. Social media
3. Events/seminars/speaking
4. Client communication and client retention
5. Trade shows and conference sponsorships

Marketing Channel #1 — Your website — The key to your marketing efforts

There are many marketing channels you can use to market to women. One of the most important is your website. Women will Google you. What will they find?

Go to your computer right now and Google yourself. What came up? Women will research you and your company online, so this is crucially important.

All of your marketing materials should point to your website for more information. I know some of you are restricted in what you can put up online, but make every effort to make sure your online footprint represents you well.

Here's a list of what content should be on your website:

- About us page
- Services you provide
- Client testimonials
- Client survey results
- What to bring to your first meeting
- Updated headshot
- Contact information
- Blog

About us page

Here's what to include in your About us page (Hint: these also apply to your social media profiles):

- Your credentials — Are you an authority? Do you specialize in a certain area? Do you have certifications or degrees? Have you worked or are you working for a well known company? Include anything that lets her know you are competent and knowledgeable.
- A picture — Include a professional headshot or a shot of you and your staff.
- Who you work with — This is missing from a lot of bios and profiles I review, yet it is crucial. Is there a minimum amount of investable assets someone needs in order to work with you? Do you work mainly with high net-worth individuals? Do you work with middle-class families? How many clients do you currently have? (If you limit your practice to a smaller number, let people know that and how you can offer more personal service because of it.) Do you work with a specialized group: Divorced women, doctors, special need families, 65 plus, etc.? Let people know that you are a good fit for their situation.
- A personal story — Why did you get into the business? What are you passionate about? (No, I'm not talking about skiing or golf.) Are there any charitable organizations you work with? Most profiles are incredibly dull and dry. You can have a personality and still be professional. Even just throw in a favorite quote. Give prospects some idea of what you are like as a

person. (See Chapter 9 — Referrals — How to Generate Word of Mouth for more ideas on this subject.)

On my website www.thesoccermommyth.com, I use this quote: *"Inside every older person is a younger person wondering what the hell happened"* — Cora Harvey Armstrong. I also use this quote, *"Life shrinks or expands in proportion to one's courage."* Anais Nin. You'd be surprised how many people comment on those quotes.

Bottom line, do something, anything, to stand out from the rest of the pack.

Services you provide

So many websites are vague about the services the company or individual offers — *wealth management, financial planning services* — what does that mean? Get specific about the services you offer like: retirement planning, estate planning, asset protection strategies, long-term care planning, tax reduction strategies, business succession planning, etc.

Client testimonials

Whenever possible, use testimonials from your clients. Women especially want to know what it's like to work with you. They want to hear from other clients like themselves.

A great time to ask for a client testimonial is at the end of a review meeting. Remember the two questions designed to generate testimonials and referrals?

1. If there was one thing I could change about how we work together that would improve our relationship, what would it be?
2. What do you like the best about working together?

Watch the testimonials flow out of your clients' mouths. Take notes and ask them if you can share their thoughts. Women especially will say "yes" if they genuinely think you're doing a good job.

Testimonial tip #1

Here's a tip to dramatically increase the quality of your testimonials from Laura Posey. Laura is the Chief Instigator at Dancing Elephants, a company that specializes in dramatically growing profits for entrepreneurs. Laura's expertise is in finding areas of your business that should be 10 times more profitable and getting those profits in the bank.

Getting quality testimonials from your clients can be tough. It's not that they don't want to recommend you, it is usually that they just aren't used to writing glowing reviews. Your client may be thinking, "John is amazing. I can't imagine trusting my financial future to anyone else. He's become a part of our family." But when they write it down it comes out, "John is a very good financial advisor, and I like him a lot."

To get great testimonials, I recommend writing them yourself and asking your client to approve them. Here's how you set it up:

"Roxanne, you've mentioned that you enjoy working with me, and I wonder if you'd share your experience with others. I know you are busy so I thought it might help if I write up how our experience together has gone and then you can edit and add anything you think is relevant. That way you don't have to start with a blank sheet of paper. Would that be okay?"

Using this technique you'll get the quality testimonials you want without putting a burden on your clients to be excellent writers.

Thanks Laura. You can also apply this technique to the "What could I do to improve our relationship? What do you like best about working together?" question scenario. As your client shares answers to the second question, take notes. Type it up and send it to them and ask if you can use it as a testimonial. Again, this way your client is not facing a blank sheet of paper.

Testimonial tip #2

Alison Silbert, author of *"Boost Your Revenues By Turning People Away — How to Sell More To Your Ideal Client Online"* has another powerful testimonial tip.

"Paint a 'before and after' picture. Outline the client's situation before he/she came to you for help, state what you did to improve the client's situation and any benefits/improvements the client experienced once the change was implemented."

I'd also add to this, if the client had any concerns coming in to you, what did you do to address those concerns? Here's an example:

"My previous advisor didn't communicate very often with my husband and me. I never really understood his investment strategy and some of the investment products he pushed. So I walked into my first meeting with (financial advisor) expecting much of the same — a bunch of technical jargon and pie charts that didn't make much sense. To my great surprise, (financial advisor) talked to my husband and me in plain English. He took a genuine interest in our lives and learning about our family. He took the time to answer all my questions, and he checks in on a regular basis. For the first time in my life I feel like I have a financial advisor who actually knows me and who I can trust to have my best interests at heart."

Client survey results

A smart tactic for gathering not only testimonials but valuable feedback is to do a client survey. You can include some of the highlights from that survey on your website. For example, Mary Moose at Victory Wealth Management asked her clients a powerful question then shared the results on her website. She asked her clients whether they agreed that Victory Wealth Management cared more about them than their money. The results were unanimous. "100% of our clients agree we care more about them than their money." What an awesome question, and what a powerful statement that result sends to Mary's current and future clients!

Check out the Victory Wealth Management website at www. victorywmi.com.

What to bring to your first meeting

Provide a bullet point list of the documents and information new clients should bring to the first meeting. This allows women to feel prepared, which is especially important for Deliberate Debbie and Traditional Tess. Be sure to state clearly that all information will remain confidential.

Updated headshot

C'mon people. I see some head shots that look like they're left over from the '80s. Yeah, you're a little older and a little grayer now. That's OK. It adds character. (At least that's what they tell me). Your head-shot needs to look like you.

Contact information, office hours and location with directions

This sounds like a no-brainer, but I'm always surprised at how many websites and marketing materials hide this information. Put it front and center on your home page.

Blog

A blog can be a part of your website or can have a separate online location. I recommend you make it a part of your website so your visitors can see all your information in one place.

A blog allows you to constantly update your website with posts about subject matter your clients care about. Don't know what to write? Start with the most common questions your clients ask you. Make a list of the questions, then create a post that answers each question individually. This is the perfect place to show your expertise and give readers a chance to get to know more about you. A blog also gives your readers a chance to interact with you in the comment section.

Your blog can be the center of your website strategy and also your social media strategy.

Marketing Channel #2 — Social Media

The world of social media is gaining a lot of attention from financial professionals. So I've brought in an expert to talk to you about the opportunities for individuals and companies in the financial services industry.

Amy McIlwain is the President of Financial Social Media, www.financialsocialmedia.com. Financial Social Media specifically addresses the compliance issues surrounding social media and the financial industry. With her unique background in both online marketing and financial services, Amy knows which media vehicles work and the marketing language needed to deliver results.

Take it away, Amy.

Why should I use social media?

The staggering growth of social media in the past year should be evidence enough of the reasons that every individual, especially in the business spectrum, should be participating in the conversations taking place online.

The great thing about social media is its ability to harvest relationships between users. A relationship, either between two individuals or between an individual and a company, should be treated the same. Social media acts as the perfect social and cultural context in which relationships can be built and nurtured.

Social networking campaigns can also be used as a low-cost, high-impact way of positioning a business or individual as a thought-leader and industry expert. This will in turn open doors for business development such as leads, referrals, inquiries and most importantly, sales. Posting content that not only demonstrates expertise, but also creates relationships with followers and fans will help you grow your business.

Social media can help you:

- Prospect for new clients
- Gain referrals
- Build upon existing client relations
- Increase sales
- Create brand awareness
- Manage your brand representation
- Recruit new hires
- Learn about new technologies and competitors

Which social media tools and platforms are best for prospecting new clients, and which are best for building relationships with existing clients?

While there are a myriad of social networking services and tools, I've broken down the field into the top three, detailing what main purposes they serve and how they can benefit your social media strategy.

Social Networking Services

- **LinkedIn.** LinkedIn is a top professional networking community. The proliferation of LinkedIn as a professional resource for individuals and businesses to connect and expand their social networks has led to its exponential growth (100% in the past year). LinkedIn is the place to go if you're looking to network with other top professionals in your field, generate leads to intercept potential prospects and build upon existing client relations. It's also a great place to share your expertise and position yourself as the expert in your field.
- **Facebook.** Before you make any predisposed judgments about Facebook, I'd like to point out the strong business trend on Facebook this past year. Facebook is no longer just a personal networking site. With the proliferation of fan pages (yes, they are still called fan pages) came the explosion of businesses using

Facebook to their advantage. Facebook fan pages have given organizations the ability to create an online community representing their brand, its values and mission. It gives organizations a chance to start conversations and interact directly with their customers. The real kicker of Facebook is its ability to go viral and spread information extremely fast. News, discussions, links and photos can circulate across the Facebook grid with the ease of the "share" button, allowing businesses to expose their brand to a multitude of people with the simple click of the "like" button.

- **Twitter.** Even more than Facebook, Twitter's ability to circulate information quickly is a bit of an understatement. The best way to view your company's engagement with Twitter is presenting yourself as a content DJ. With a 140-character limit and a different audience at all times, it's crucial that you use Twitter to post attention-getting and engaging content. It's also key that you stay engaged with your followers and continue to put out great information. Twitter can be a great prospecting tool for generating leads. The combination of a diverse audience with a quick circulation rate can expose your content to new people and different networks.

What content should I create, and what should I be writing about?

The more quality content you post to your networks, the more users you will attract to your site. Write about your area of expertise. Answer your client's most frequently asked questions, point to online articles that will be of interest to your audience, share great content from the people you follow, and use Twitter or Facebook to link to your blog posts. And don't forget to join the conversation. You may have a large amount of followers and be kicking out great content on a daily basis, but until you start jumping into the conversation with your users you won't see a great return. Make it a priority to engage with your users on a daily basis by sharing, commenting and liking their posts.

What compliance issues do I have to deal with (as an individual and as a company)?

If you or your business already has a social media policy in place, review your organization's existing policies first, then consider the following rules of engagement.

Rules of Engagement
* Be judicious — Know and follow your organization's code of conduct and privacy policy.
* Be transparent — Represent and identify your company truthfully.
* Be responsible — Know your role and stick to your area of expertise. Don't overstep your bounds.
* Be a leader — Don't denigrate competitors, let alone your organization.

Great advice. Thanks Amy. For more ideas on how to use social media, go to www.SellingFinancialServicesToWomen.com

Marketing Channel #3 — Events/Seminars/Speaking

A key component of your marketing strategy should be to get out in front of people to do presentations. I've talked with many advisors who feel this is the single most profitable prospecting activity they do.

I don't have to tell you that right now people are desperate for financial information, especially women.

I'll repeat a list of seminar topics from Chapter 6 — How to Sell to Women, plus a few more. The more specific you are with your seminar topics, the better.

* How to teach kids about money

- How men and women can talk to each other about money (great for newlyweds as well as married couples)
- Sandwiched caregivers — who takes care of the caregiver?
- The four biggest mistakes in retirement planning
- Beyond the 401K — what you need to know about investing
- Financial planning for business owners
- The four financial keys to setting up a successful business
- Everything you always wanted to know but were afraid to ask your financial advisor
- Caring for aging parents — do you know what insurance your parents have?
- The new health care law — how it will affect your financial planning
- How to get started when your financial life is in a shoe box
- The myth of Prince Charming — what young women need to know about financial planning
- Financial Security University
- How to stay on top of the stock market but still be able to sleep at night
- Estate planning — how to keep the government from getting your money
- Guaranteed income for life — how to live a cat-food free life and never run out of money
- The three biggest financial mistakes women make when getting a divorce
- Alternative investments — beyond stocks, bonds and mutual funds
- Are you over-insured or under-insured?

The reason these seminars and events are so powerful is they allow you to get in front of large groups of new prospects. There are three main ways to set up these events:

1. Invite your current clients and ask them to bring a friend. This way you provide added value to your current clients, but also get in front of new people. It can be as simple as a

lunch-and-learn event in your office conference room, or as elaborate as renting out space in a local hotel or event center.

2. Ask to speak at events put on by other organizations. Is there a business organization, senior organization, women's organization, or church organization that puts on regular meetings? Ask to speak. Share the topics you can speak about and why those topics are of interest to their audience or members.

3. Partner with someone else to produce an event. I know an advisor who partnered with a local Lexus dealer. The Lexus dealer invited all of his female clients (and told them to bring a friend). The advisor invited all of his female clients (and also asked them to bring a friend). They held an after-hours event at the Lexus dealership where the women got to test drive the new hybrid model. The advisor did a short seminar on finances and how they could afford that new Lexus. Both partners had female clients from similar economic backgrounds, so it was a perfect match, and both walked away with new business.

When you speak, always try to allow at least 5-10 minutes for Q&A and stick around afterwards to talk with people. (I know this sounds obvious, but I've seen too many presenters finish, shut down their equipment and head straight for the door.)

And let me address the guys who are saying, "I'd love to speak at a women's event, but do women's groups allow male speakers?" The answer is almost always, "Yes." And let me tell you, men get huge credit for showing up and engaging with women's groups. You must be genuine about your interest. I know an insurance agent who was raised by a single mom. He loves to get up in front of women's groups and tell the story of how his mom is his hero. He always walks away with business.

My dad was always a big believer in promoting women. He'd tell tales of being surrounded by women with a wife and twin daughters.

(We had him well-trained.) By sharing stories about the women in his life and how much he loved them, he gained credibility with the women he worked with. You can, too.

Marketing Channel #4 — Client communication and client retention

Don't forget to market to your current clients! Client retention should be a key part of any marketing strategy. Remember the research about how women remain very loyal to advisors with whom they have a good relationship. How do you maintain that relationship?

We know that one of the main things women want from financial professionals is more communication. So here are some ways to share information, build stronger relationships and retain more clients.

Email — Send updates on your strategy, portfolio changes or market recaps. Send invitations to client appreciation or learning events. Include a line at the bottom reminding clients to pass along your name to people looking for a financial advisor.

Newsletters — What's going on in the market, what are people concerned about, what are some of the most common questions you get from clients? Put the answers in a short monthly or quarterly newsletter and encourage your clients to pass it along to their friends. The key here is to keep it short and sweet. No one has time to read a 10 page newsletter. Focus on one topic if possible.

Snail mail — In today's online world, an old-fashioned card in the mail gets noticed. Send greeting cards, especially birthday cards in the mail. If possible, include some small gift, even just a $5 Starbucks card for a free cup of coffee. When your client pulls out that gift card, it gives them an opportunity to think or talk about you. When you get a new client, send a handwritten thank you note. Women especially will value this more than you know.

Women's Advisory Boards

If you really want to do a good job of communicating with women (your current clients or other women in the community) and delivering the experience they desire, include women in the creation of that experience. A terrific way to do that is to create a Women's Advisory Board.

Gerry Myers is CEO, president and co-founder of Advisory Link which specializes in marketing and selling more effectively to women consumers as well as helping corporations recruit, retain and promote female employees. She is also author of *Targeting the New Professional Woman: How to Market and Sell to Today's 57 Million Working Women.* Gerry has helped many financial institutions develop their own Women's Advisory Boards across the country, including more than a dozen for MassMutual Financial Group and six for New York Life Insurance Company.

So what is a Women's Advisory Board and why should you create one? I'll let you hear directly from Gerry Myers.

The best way to develop strategies and materials that will attract women is to ask them what they want. While focus groups provide some answers to marketing questions, women in focus groups frequently say what they think the host organization wants to hear. Often they don't have enough in-depth information to provide the best advice to the company. A Women's Advisory Board (WAB) can change all that. Women's Advisory Boards are the best and most cost-effective marketing tool a company can have if they are created and facilitated correctly. That, of course, is the secret to their success.

Focusing on the women's market by allowing your ideal clients to tell you what they want, what they will buy and how best to reach them is the heart of a Women's Advisory Board created by Advisory Link. The soul of the board is determined by the women selected to serve on it. A WAB is a flexible vehicle that can:

- Reach powerful, well-connected and influential women and their key networks.
- Teach the importance of the women's market, and how to most effectively target women by finding out what they do and don't want.
- Serve as an ongoing focus group to recommend and critique marketing strategies, advertising campaigns, collateral materials, sales tools, websites, social media tactics and promotional offers.
- Provide access to strong advocates and diverse markets in the women's community for your company and brand.
- Introduce new ideas that will strategically expand your business.
- Increase sales through a network of dedicated women.
- Monitor the community's perception of your company, the competition, etc.
- Provide strategies for recruitment and referrals.
- Assist in revising policies and procedures that will help develop and promote women within your organization.
- Mentor female employees.
- Represent your company as Ambassadors of Goodwill.
- Host in-house functions, charity events and select corporate meetings.

Gerry Myers' clients have had great success with their Women's Advisory Boards. Tap into the power of these influential women and the insight they can bring to your organization. Use those insights to improve your client communication and overall client experience AND your bottom line.

ACTION STEPS:

* Have a website or some online presence that lets her know who you are, what services you offer and who you work with.
* Google yourself to see what shows up. Make sure all information is up-to-date.
* Ask for client testimonials. Use the two review meeting questions to discover what your clients like about working with you, and what they feel can be improved upon.
* Have a marketing plan and be consistent in your messaging across all marketing channels.
* Speak and present as much as possible. Partner with other professionals and approach groups and associations in your area with specific seminar ideas.
* Schedule regular communication with your existing clients.
* Consider creating a Women's Advisory Board to help guide your marketing to women efforts and connect with important women in the community.

Marketing Channel #5 — Trade shows and conference sponsorships

Some of you may participate in or sponsor trade shows and conferences. The question is, how do you get your money's worth out of these events? How do you get prospects to actually stop at your booth and participate with you and your staff? Here are some ideas.

Book signings. When I speak at conferences, usually for a client, I sign books afterwards at my client's booth. At the end of the session, I announce that my client has generously purchased X number of books to give out at their booth. I invite attendees to stop by after my talk to pick up their signed copy. This works beautifully. While other vendors stand around with nearly empty booths, my client has a line of people. While I sign books, my clients work the lines discussing products and setting up appointments. If you're not an author, or don't have an author who can speak for you, buy copies of a popular business book. Financial professionals love free books.

Charity tie-in. At a recent mom blogger event I attended, a vendor donated $1 for every business card collected to Save the Children. If you're at an event, see if there is a local charity you can work with, or pick a national charity. One of my favorites is Dress for Success, www.dressforsuccess.org. They provide professional attire and career training for women trying to build a better life. The charitable tie-in can be a great conversation starter and a chance to share your company values.

Have a question displayed prominently at your booth. Use a question like, "What are the two biggest threats to your retirement portfolio?" Our brains are drawn to questions and solving puzzles. People will stop to throw out answers. It's a great conversation starter, especially if you're selling annuities or long-term care insurance, since we know outliving your money and a major health event are two of the biggest threats to our retirement.

Follow up piece. When I speak, I like to have a follow-up piece I can send to my audience, usually a pdf of a handout with some original research, or copies of key slides in my presentation. It's a way to follow up with attendees and offer them something of value. For example, after my presentation on "The Four Types of Women Investors," I offered to send a summary report of the four types to the attendees. My client and I were stopped throughout the rest of the conference by attendees wanting to make sure they would get that report. The email with the report also gave my client a chance to remind the attendees of the specific product they were talking about at the conference. It was a total win-win.

NOTE: Some conferences have specific rules about gathering or using attendee contact information. Double check with conference organizers to see what is allowed.

ACTION STEPS:

* Give attendees a reason to stop by your booth (book signing or free books).
* Send out a follow up note or email after the conference with a value added report, tips or information.

CONCLUSION:

Understand which images and what language will appeal specifically to women. Include women in your marketing creation and reviews. Make sure you have a strong online presence, since that's where so many women today are spending their time and doing their financial research. Get comfortable speaking in front of groups and share your knowledge and expertise with a room full of prospects. And find new and better ways to start or continue conversations with women when you're speaking at or attending trade shows. Use these proven techniques to attract new female clients and customers.

Once you meet these women, what should you talk about? What do women care about when it comes to money and financial planning? Find out in the full report on my Women and Finance Survey.

WOMEN AND FINANCE SURVEY RESULTS

In this chapter, I'll provide an overview of the most interesting insights from my Women and Finance Study.

I had two terrific partners in this research:

1. **Alpha Mom**, www.alphamom.com, was my partner for surveying women under 50, especially moms. Alpha Mom is a consumer lifestyle brand, new media and research company for moms and moms-to-be. It was founded and is run by the fabulous Isabel Kallman.

2. **Vibrant Nation,** www.vibrantnation.com, was my partner for surveying women over 50. Vibrant Nation is the leading online community for women 50 plus. Stephen Reily, Vibrant Nation founder and CEO, knows more than any man should about Boomer women. His interest and engagement with this group is inspiring.

Here's how women responded to our women and finance questions.

And, the survey says..........

Do you have a financial advisor?

WOMEN UNDER 50	WOMEN OVER 50
Yes — 26.5%	Yes — 51%
No — 73.5%	No — 49%

These numbers should be encouraging to financial advisors. A lot of women do not have an advisor, but are actively looking for financial guidance.

How did you find him or her?

WOMEN UNDER 50	WOMEN OVER 50
Referral from friend/family — 54.2%	Referral from friend/family — 45%
Professional referral — 25.4%	Professional referral — 29%
Other options — 15.3%	Other options — 23%
Internet — 5.1%	Internet — 3%

It's no surprise that women are finding their financial advisors through referrals, mainly referrals from their friends and families.

Why did you choose to work with him/her?
Choose your top 3 reasons.

Both women under and over 50 had the same answers:
1. Felt a personal connection/trust/respect
2. Came referred by a trusted source
3. Worked for a reputable firm/company
4. Successful track record
5. Training/certification/credentials

Notice that the top reasons are all about trust, connection, relationships and referrals from trusted sources. In other words, everything we've been focusing on in this book.

Who do financial advisors focus their attention on — men or women?

WOMEN UNDER 50	WOMEN OVER 50
Men — 63.9%	Men — 59%
Men and women equally — 33.1%	Men and women equally — 39%
Women — 3%	Women — 2%

Even if you think you're doing a good job of including women and focusing your attention on them, double check yourself. Really pay attention to how much time you focus on her vs. him. If she's not engaging with you during the meeting, ask her questions, ask about her concerns and draw her into the conversation. If you don't engage her directly, she may think you are purposefully ignoring her.

If you could change one thing about the way you work with your financial advisor, what would it be?

In this open ended question the top answer was **more communication**.

I want more personal contact so that he understands my life and priorities
I would be in touch with him more often
More opportunities for check-in
Would like to see him more often
That he check in with us more often
Don't meet with her enough

More regular communication
More contact throughout the year
Regularly scheduled meetings to discuss plans
I would discuss more things with him
More time to meet with her
More interaction
Personalized conversations on a more regular basis
I would like more touch points with my advisor

The second most popular answer was **education**:
He would give better explanations
I would have more knowledge about investing
I would put more time into educating myself
Less jargon in his advice
More explanation about alternative options
Understand the logistics of the trading that is done
I'd like more knowledge
I'd like more access to ask quick questions
He'd help me make more smart decisions

Use the action steps in this book to be a better communicator. And understand the importance of providing education and information to your female clients and female audiences.

What financial issues are you most concerned about?

WOMEN UNDER 50	WOMEN OVER 50
1. Feeling financially secure	1. Feeling financially secure
2. Retirement planning	2. Having a comprehensive plan in place
3. Getting out of debt	3. Retirement planning
4. Having a comprehensive plan in place	4. Outliving your money

WOMEN UNDER 50	WOMEN OVER 50
5. Outliving your money	5. Getting out of debt
6. Socially responsible investing	6. Wealth management
7. Wealth management	7. Socially responsible investing

Make sure you are targeting your marketing material and your client presentations to what each group cares about most.

What does having money allow you to do?

WOMEN UNDER 50	WOMEN OVER 50
1. Provide for your family	1. Take care of yourself and the people you love
2. Take care of yourself and the people you love	2. Not have to rely on others
3. Prepare for the future	3. Prepare for the future
4. Protect your family	4. Achieve financial independence
5. Plan for your future	5. Plan for your future
6. Not have to rely on others	6. Be responsible
7. Be responsible	7. Provide for your family
8. Achieve financial independence	8. Protect your family
9. Keep your promises	9. Keep your promises

Be aware that many women under 50 are bearing or sharing the responsibility for providing for their families. Remember to make sure she has enough life insurance. And help your clients 50 plus find ways to not be a burden or to have to rely on others. Help both groups feel more prepared. ("Prepared" is a great word to use in your marketing copy and sales presentations.)

Were you raised to believe:

WOMEN UNDER 50	WOMEN OVER 50
You have to take control over your own finances —78.7 %	You have to take control over your own finances — 56%
A man will take care of you financially — 21.3%	A man will take care of you financially — 44%

What do you believe now?

WOMEN UNDER 50	WOMEN OVER 50
You have to take control over your own finances — 95%	You have to take control over your own finances — 97%
A man will take care of you financially — 5%	A man will take care of you financially — 3%

These numbers surprised even me. Women, even the more traditional 50 plus group, feel they need to take responsibility for and control over their finances. Even if they were raised to believe "A man is the plan," real life experience has changed their minds.

Which article would you rather read, "The four secrets to having the retirement of your dreams" or "The four biggest mistakes in retirement planning and how to avoid them"?

WOMEN UNDER 50	WOMEN OVER 50
Biggest mistakes — 55%	Biggest mistakes — 42%
Retirement of dreams — 30%	Retirement of dreams — 30%
Neither — 15%	Neither — 28%

In both groups the majority of women wanted to read the article about avoiding financial mistakes. Test the verbiage in your ads, your articles and your seminar titles. Women may respond to prevention verbiage more than achievement verbiage.

Response to images from financial ads showing women in a subservient position

In these images from actual financial ads the woman has her head on the man's shoulder, the man is carrying the woman or the man is a visionary, looking out as the woman stands behind him.

When you see images like these in financial services ads, how do they make you feel?

WOMEN UNDER 50	WOMEN OVER 50
I don't relate to these images. I don't want to have to rely on someone else (husband or otherwise) for financial security — 50%	I don't relate to these images. I don't want to have to rely on someone else (husband or otherwise) for financial security — 78%
Loved and supported. I can rely on my husband to take care of me — 49%	Loved and supported. I can rely on my husband to take care of me — 12%
Sad. I've lost my husband and I miss him — 1%	Sad. I've lost my husband and I miss him — 10%

To see the images from the survey, go to www.SellingFinancial ServicesToWomen.com. If you are targeting women 50 plus, be especially careful of images of couples with the woman in a subordinate position. While they may work for men, they may backfire for women.

Images from financial services ads women responded to most positively:
1. Multi-generational family
2. Multi-generational group of three women
3. Professional woman
4. Couple but on an equal level

To see these images go to www.SellingFinancialServicesTo Women.com. In both the under 50 and over 50 groups, the most favored images were the group of three women and the family shots. If you are targeting women, use these types of images in your marketing material. Remember if you have established your Women's Advisory Group you can get their feedback.

ACTION STEPS:

✳ Increase your referral efforts. The vast majority of women in the survey found their advisor through a referral.

✳ Provide more communication and more educational opportunities. These were the two things women wished for most.

✳ In your sales and marketing materials, focus on ways you can make her feel financially secure. Focus on how you can help her feel protected and prepared.

✳ In your sales and marketing materials, focus on how money can help her take care of herself and the people she loves.

✳ For women under 50, focus on their roles as providers for themselves and their families.

✳ For women 50 plus, beware of images of couples where the woman is in a subservient position.

CONCLUSION:

There are some traits women of all ages share when it comes to their feelings about money. But we also found some distinct differences between women under 50 and women over 50. Make sure you are tailoring your marketing materials and sales pitches to the needs and desires of each group.

A foolproof way to connect with all women is to ask great questions and listen to their answers. One of the most powerful tools in this book is the following list of women-winning questions.

THE CLIENT MEETING —
WOMEN-WINNING QUESTIONS

You're meeting with a woman or a couple. It could be a prospecting call, a sales call, a new client meeting or a meeting with an existing client. What does that meeting look like? What questions should you ask? Here's a step-by-step look at what actions to take and what questions to ask to increase your chances of success. We'll start with the client meeting itself, then move on to women-winning questions

The Client Meeting

Step One — Meeting Confirmation
Before the meeting, make sure you have her email address. If it is a couple, make sure you have both email addresses. Send an email before the meeting which should include:
* A confirmation of the appointment time and location. If it is at your office, include specific directions.
* The length of the meeting. This way you will both allot the appropriate amount of time to have a successful meeting.
* Your bio. Women want to know who you are and would love to have this information before the meeting. (For more information on what to include in your bio, see Chapter 6 — How to Sell to Women.)

- Your contact information including phone numbers which she can call should she need more specific directions.
- An agenda for the meeting. Men want to know the goal of the meeting. Women want to prepare ahead of time for any questions or information you might need.
- A link to your website where she can gather more information if she needs it.

Step Two — Your Client's Introduction
- Ask her about herself — "Tell me a little bit about yourself. Tell me about your family, your responsibilities, your passions." (Take notes, especially of family names, where's she's from, interests, job, etc.)
- Ask her and her husband what they'd each like to get out of the meeting today.
- Ask your clients what they've heard about you. Their answers can help you do a better job of selling to them. If they're very familiar with you, you may need to do less selling and move more quickly to the close. If they mention something specific, like your investment strategy, you know that is of interest to them and can focus on it. (Asking this question also gives you a chance to clear up any misinformation they may have about you.)

Step Three — Your Introduction
(Note: many advisors reverse step two and three. Be sure to start with your client introduction first. This way you can customize what you say based on what you already know about them.)
- Re-affirm the time frame for the meeting — "Is this time frame still good for you?"
- Explain what you do.
- Share your credentials.
- Explain how you get paid.
- Explain who you work with.
- Give some personal information — Tell them where you're

from. If you have a family photo, point to it and introduce your family members. Share why you got into the business, or what you enjoy most about your job (helping clients build a smart, comprehensive financial plan, seeing a long-term care policy help keep a loved one in their home rather than a nursing home, helping parents send their kids to college, etc.)

Step Four — Women-Winning Questions

This is the step where you ask excellent questions, sit back and listen. These questions work especially well with women clients. We'll get to those questions in just a minute.

Step Five — Tie Solutions to Stated Needs

Tie products/solutions to your client's specifically stated goals/problems/concerns (if the purpose of the meeting is a specific sale). OR — Explain in more detail what it would look like to work together (if you are still in the prospecting stage).

* Include a more in-depth explanation of your investment strategy.
* Explain how you make product recommendations and why.

Step Six — Meeting Wrap

* First and foremost, do not EVER go over your allotted meeting time. If it looks like you are running out of time, tell your clients you want to respect their time and realize your allotted time is running out. Ask if they have the ability to continue for a specified amount of time, or set up another meeting to finish up the discussion.
* End the meeting with a summary of what you've learned about the clients. Make sure you are clear on their needs and priorities.
* Ask if she has any questions you haven't answered or any concerns you have not addressed.
* Set up a second meeting. She may need more time to think about what you've said, go over material, do her own research

and talk with trusted friends and family members. Remember, if she says she needs more time, she is NOT saying "No." Just make sure you have a second meeting set up before she leaves.

• Ask if anyone else is going to be involved in the decision making. If you're an FA, find out who else might be involved in the choice of an advisor. Remember The Brother-In-Law Effect. If she has a relative, CPA or other trusted partner in decision making, you want that person or those people in the room. You don't ever want to rely on someone else (your client) to explain your strategy or story. Too many sales are lost that way.

Step Seven — Follow Up
• Send an immediate email thanking her for her time, whether she's decided to work with you or not. This can and should be very short and sweet. If you've set up a second meeting, include that information in the email for her records. You can send out correspondence later with action plans. This email is designed to show your responsiveness and attention to follow up.
• If you've sold her a product, like an insurance product, follow up a week or two later just to check in, see if she has any questions, remind her of the specific need this product addresses and thank her for her business. This is also a time to bring up referrals.

Women-Winning Questions

Here's a list of powerful questions to ask all of your clients. Women will especially appreciate these questions.

Introduction stage:
• Have you worked with a financial planner/insurance agent/ bank before? What did you like and not like about that experience? OR What was your best and worst experience with your previous advisor?
• Where are you from?

* Who are the important people in your life, both two-legged and four-legged? (Use this question if you think she has a pet. Pet lovers will appreciate this question.)
* Who is affected by your financial decisions?
* Are you responsible for your parent's care or finances?
* In what ways are you responsible for your family? (This is a great question for stay-at-home moms since it avoids the "What do you do?" question that most people answer by stating what they do for work. I find the "What do you do?" question puts stay-at-home moms on the defensive.)
* Was there a catalyst, something that prompted you to reach out to me?
* Who do you trust to give you financial advice?
* What are your sources for financial information?
* What kinds of opportunities are you looking for?
* How have you gathered the wealth you have?

Financial planning/selling stage:
* How big a role do you want to play in the investment decisions? Do you want to be involved in the overall planning only, or do you want an active part in the day-to-day decisions?
* How do you make financial decisions?
* (If it's a couple) How do you make financial decisions? Whose decision is usually the tie breaker?
* What does being financially OK mean to each of you?
* What's keeping you up at night?
* What's the smartest financial decision you've ever made?
* What are your short-term and long-term goals?
* If we were to work together, and it's now 12 months later, looking back a year, what did I do for you?
* What did you learn about money from your parents?
* What was your best and worst experience with money?
* What's the one thing you absolutely do not want to happen?
* What do you want out of this relationship? What do you expect from me as an advisor?

- Do you have any concerns we didn't cover?
- Have I answered all your questions?
- Is there anything else?

Current client/relationship building stage:
- What's the one thing I could change that would improve our working relationship?
- How do you feel about the decisions we made? Are you comfortable with them?
- Are there any important people in your life (adult children, aging parents, trusted advisors) you feel it would be important for me to meet?
- What causes are you most passionate about? How do you handle philanthropic giving?
- If you had more financial freedom what personal or professional passions would you pursue?
- Is there anything I can say or do to allay your concerns?
- What's going on in your world? Have there been any changes? How is everyone's health? Have your caregiving responsibilities changed? Are there any big occasions coming up?

I'm sure you can add more questions to this list. The reason these questions are so powerful is because they are designed to get your clients talking about what *they* care about (especially your female clients). These questions are also designed to pull out key information that will help you do a better job of meeting your clients' needs and delivering service the way they want it delivered. Asking these questions and incorporating the answers into your planning will help you retain more clients.

Questions NOT to ask women

Note that there are two types of questions that tend to backfire with women:
  * Challenging questions
  * Set-up questions

Challenging question example: **You say you're pretty knowledgeable about investing. How did you do in the last bear market?** In the business world, I see men asking challenging questions all the time. It's a way to get a one-up position, gain respect and show your expertise. But this may not work with women. Set off her "threat" meter and you destroy her trust.

Set-up question example: **If I could show you something clearly superior to what you currently have, would you make a change today?** Remember women's longer decision making cycle. She doesn't want to feel forced to commit to any decision until she's had time to think it through.

What to do with the answers/information you've gathered

So you've asked great questions, and either yourself or someone on your team has taken note of the answers. What do you do with this information?

Have a database or CRM system (Customer Relationship Management system) where you store information about clients. You want to be able to sort clients by certain attributes. (Learn about just such a system at www.SellingFinancialServicesToWomen.com)

For example, The University of Richmond Spiders have just won a national championship. (Yes, U of R is my alma mater, and yes, our mascot really is a spider. Those of you with unusual mascots, say the UC Santa Cruz Banana Slugs, can relate.) You can pull up your clients who are University of Richmond grads and send them a congratulatory note.

Note: Be aware of your clients' religious faiths and be sure you are sending appropriate holiday cards.

If you have clients who are golfers, readers or Boston Terrier lovers, you can send them more appropriate gifts (a company golf shirt, gift certificate to Barnes & Noble or Snausages).

ACTION STEPS:

✳ Follow the above guidelines for client meetings.
✳ Ask women-winning questions in your meetings and hear and act upon her answers.

CONCLUSION:

Help her prepare ahead of time for client meetings and follow up quickly. And ask the above questions. Simply asking these questions and actively listening to the answers (see tips on active listening in Chapter 6 — How to Sell to Women) will help you close more business and grow stronger relationships.

And that's what it's all about.

14

CONCLUSION

I hope this book has inspired you to focus, or renew your focus on women. My goal is for everyone who reads this book to walk away with at least three ideas they can implement immediately to grow their business.

Women are a growing economic force, they are participating more in financial decision making and they are actively looking for financial guidance. Unfortunately, many women have not found someone they trust to provide that guidance. Be that person. Understand her buying process. Use her preferred communication style. Build a long-term relationship.

The opportunities are out there. This is your chance to break away from the pack and seize the day.

Doing a better job with women isn't just the right thing to do — it's the smart thing to do.

Many of you may be thinking, "This is all great stuff, but where do I begin?" Here are seven action steps to start with.

The Seven Most Important Action Steps:

1. Look at your top client list. If there are couples on that list, make sure you have a relationship with the wife. Invite her to a review meeting. Set up coffee or a lunch where you can simply ask her about her life. Get her email address and phone number and include her in your client communications.

2. Sit down with your female clients (either single or part of a couple) and ask them two questions: What is the one thing I could change that would improve our relationship? What do you like best about working together? The first question gives her permission to be open with you about anything she may not be satisfied with. It will clue you in to any ways you are not connecting with her. The second question is designed to focus on what she likes best and will generate testimonials on the spot. Ask permission to use these testimonials in your marketing materials.

3. Look through the Women-Winning Questions list and choose three questions to ask all of your female clients.

4. Practice one of the four listening techniques:
    * The power of the pause
    * WAIT — why am I talking
    * Give less advice — ask better questions
    * Don't jump in and try to solve her problems before she's had a chance to articulate them

5. Set up an educational seminar event. Survey your current clients (send out an email to your client list) and give them three financial topics to choose from. Do a seminar on the most popular topic and make it a "bring a friend" event. (This seminar can be for women only or for both men and women.) If possible, partner with someone else so you can market the event to both of your lists — a CPA, attorney, physician, car dealership owner — anyone who has a similar client base and with whom you think your clients would have a positive experience.

6. Ask your female clients what groups or organizations they belong to, and if those groups would be interested in having you come and answer their financial questions.

7. Develop your own personal story that tells prospective clients:
    * Who you work with
    * How you help those people create better lives
    * Why you do what you do (why you got into the business)

Final thoughts

I'll leave you with this story.

I was doing a seminar in Atlanta, and there were a bunch of young guys who were new to the business in the back of the room. You know the kind of guys I'm talking about — full of bravado, yucking it up, dressed in nice suits and fancy ties. I figured they got into the business with dreams of expensive cars and big bonuses.

So I asked one of them, "What do you do, and why did you get into the business?"

He told me he had just started in long-term care insurance sales. When I followed up with the question about why he got into the business, this was his answer: "My grandmother meant everything to me. She raised me. She was my rock. After she died, we found out she was abused in the nursing home where she spent her final years. I'm in this business because it is my *mission* to make sure that never happens to anyone else's grandmother."

The whole room went quiet. Let me tell you, I looked at this guy with new respect. I felt an instant connection with him. That's the power of an authentic story. I asked him to share that story with every new prospect he meets.

I love this story because it illustrates the most crucial piece of information about why women and men buy: **People don't buy what you do — they buy why you do it.**

I've worked with thousands of financial professionals. You care. You care deeply about doing a good job for your clients. I hope the information in this book will help you share your story, better communicate with *all* of your clients and be more successful personally as well as professionally.

I look forward to hearing your success stories.

NOTES

PREFACE

1. "Financial Experience & Behaviors Among Women" Prudential Financial 2010

2. US Demographics 2010 www.census.gov/population/socdemo/statbriefs /agebrief.html (Accessed June 19, 2011).

3. Reshma Kapadia, "Why Women Get a Raw Deal on Retirement," Smart Money magazine, October, 2010, www.smartmoney.com/retirement/ planning/why-women-get-a-raw-deal-on-retirement/#tabs (Accessed June 19, 2011).

CHAPTER 1

1. Kelley M. Skoloda, *Too Busy to Shop: Marketing to Multi-Minding Women.* (Westport, CT: Praeger Publishing, 2009). p.4.

2. Mary Beth Marklein, "College Gender Gap Widens: 57% Are Women," 2005, www.usatoday.com/news/education/2005-10-19-male-college-cover_x. htm (Accessed June 19, 2011).

3. Richard Fry and D'Vera Cohn, "New Economics of Marriage: The Rise of Wives" Pew Research Center http://pewresearch.org/pubs/1466/ economics-marriage-rise-of-wives (Accessed June 19, 2011)

4. Susan B. Weiner, "Giving Women A Break," 2008, www.advisorone.com/ article/giving-women-break (Accessed June 19, 2011).

5. Rachel Bogardus Drew, "Buying For Themselves: An Analysis of Unmarried Female Home Buyers, 2006, www.jchs.harvard.edu/publica-tions/markets/n06-3_drew.pdf (Accessed June 19, 2011).

6. "Facts About The 'Purse Power' of Women," 2009 http://feck-blog. blogspot.com/2009/09/facts-about-purse-power-of-women.html (Accessed June 19, 2011).

7. Peter Damisch, Monish Kumar, Anna Zakrewski, Natalia Zhiglinskaya, Boston Consulting Group Study — Boston Consulting Group, "Leveling the Playing Field — Upgrading the Wealth Management Experience for Women," 2010 www.bcg.com/documents/file56704.pdf (Accessed June 19, 2011).

8. Amy Hiett, "Revolution in Female Charitable Giving?" 2011, Council on Foundations and Community Foundations of America www.ywc aboulder.org/wp-content/uploads/SpringYWCANewsletter2011.pdf (Accessed June 19, 2011).

9. "Key Facts About Women-Owned Businesses," www.womensbusiness researchcenter.org/research/keyfacts/ (Accessed June 19, 2011).

10. Reshma Kapadia, "Why Women Get a Raw Deal on Retirement," Smart Money magazine October, 2010, www.smartmoney.com/retirement /planning/why-women-get-a-raw-deal-on-retirement/?zone=intro message (Accessed June 19, 2011).

CHAPTER 3

1. Michael Gurian with Barbara Annis, *Leadership and the Sexes: Using Gender Science to Create Success in Business.* (San Francisco, CA: Jossey-Bass, 2008) p. xx.

2. Aaron Traister, "What Men Love About Women," http://lifestyle.msn .com/relationships/article.aspx?cp-documentid=24375124&Gt1 =32023 (Accessed June 19, 2011).

3. John Medina, *Brain Rules: 12 Principles for Surviving and Thriving at Work, Home, and School.* (Seattle, WA: Pear Press, 2008) p. 251.

4. Joseph Carrabis, "Gender Marketing Web Design Differences," 2006, www.imediaconnection.com//content//11359.asp (Accessed June 19, 2011).

5. Medina, p.247.

6. Molly Edmonds, "Do Men and Women Have Different Brains?" http:// health.howstuffworks.com/human-body/systems/nervous-system/ men-women-different-brains1.htm (Accessed June 19, 2011).

7. Jonah Lehrer, "Men vs. Women," 2009, Research study by Colin Camerer at Cal-Tech, and Read Montague, at Baylor College of Medicine http:// scienceblogs.com/cortex/2009/03/men_vs_women.php (Accessed June 19, 2001).

8. Elizabeth Pace, *The X and Y of Buy: Sell More and Market Better by Knowing How the Sexes Shop.* (Nashville, TN: Thomas Nelson, 2009) p. 37.

CHAPTER 4

1. Oppenheimer Funds, 2007 Women & Investing Survey; www.divorce mag.com/statistics/statsUS.shtm (Accessed April 16, 2007)

CHAPTER 5

1. Scott West, Mitch Anthony, *Storyselling for Financial Advisors — How Top Producers Sell.* (Dearborn Financial Publishing, 2000) p.169.

CHAPTER 6

1. West, Anthony, p. 54
2. Genworth Consumer Segmentation Study, 2007

CHAPTER 7

1. "Long Term Care Statistics," www.longtermcareinsurancetree.com/ltc-basics/long-term-care-stats.html (Accessed June 19, 2011).

CHAPTER 8

1. Reshma Kapadia, "Why Women Get a Raw Deal on Retirement," Smart Money magazine October, 2010, www.smartmoney.com/retirement/planning/why-women-get-a-raw-deal-on-retirement/?zone=intro message (Accessed June 19, 2011).
2. "The Facts of Life and Annuities," *Retirement Income Preferences,* LIMRA, 2006 Based on individuals aged 55 to 70 with at least $50,000 in household investable assets. www.limra.com/PDFs/liam/09FactofLifeConsumer.pdf (Accessed June 19, 2011).
3. 2005 Survey of Owners of Non-Qualified Annuity Contracts, conducted by The Gallup Organization and Mathew Greenwald & Associates for The Committee of Annuity Insurers, 2005.
4. "Alzheimer's disease and Long-Term Care Insurance," www.longtermcare insurancetree.com/ltc-basics/alzheimers-disease.html (Accessed June 19, 2011).
5. "Long Term Care Statistics," www.longtermcareinsurancetree.com/ltc-basics/long-term-care-stats.html (Accessed June 19, 2011).
6. Genworth Cost of Care Calculator www.genworth.com/content/gen worth/us/en/products/long_term_care/long_term_care/cost_of_care.html (Accessed June 19, 2011)

CHAPTER 9

1. Deloitte and Touche research as cited in Brand X Women and Finance research study (2011)
2. Brand X Women and Finance research study (2011)

CHAPTER 11

1. "Who's the Better Listener, Your Husband or The Dog?" Petside.com www.petside.com/article/whos-better-listener-your-husband-or-dog (Accessed June 19, 2011).

2. *Women Wealth and Giving, The Virtuous Legacy of the Boom Generation* - Margaret May Damen and Niki Nicastro McCuistion (Wiley December 21, 2009) www.womenwealthandgiving.com

RESOURCES

BOOKS

The Soccer Mom Myth, Today's Female Consumer: Who She Really Is, Why She Really Buys, Holly Buchanan and Michele Miller

Storyselling for Financial Advisors — How Top Producers Sell, Scott West & Mitch Anthony

Women Want More, Michael J. Silverstein and Kate Sayre

Leadership and The Sexes, Using Gender Science to Create Success In Business, Michael Gurian and Barbara Annis

Brain Rules, 12 Principles for Surviving and Thriving at Work, Home, and School, John Medina

The X and Y of Buy — Sell More and Market Better by Knowing How the Sexes Shop, Elizabeth Pace

Selling In A Skirt, Judy Hoberman

The Bread & Butter Chronicles, Starr Cochran

Women Wealth and Giving, The Virtuous Legacy of the Boom Generation - Margaret May Damen and Niki Nicastro McCuistion

Too Busy to Shop, Marketing to Multi-Minding Women, Kelley Skoloda

Targeting the New Professional Woman: How to Market and Sell to Today's 57 Million Working Women, Gerry Myers

Boost Your Revenues By Turning People Away — How to Sell More To Your Ideal Client Online, Alison Silbert

You Just Don't Understand, Women and Men in Conversation, Deborah Tannen

WEBSITES

www.SellingFinancialServicesToWomen.com — For more information on Holly Buchanan, tips, articles and research on selling financial services to women.

www.SpringboardEnterprises.org — Learn more about venture-catalyst Springboard Enterprises — the premier platform where entrepreneurs, investors and industry experts meet to build great women-led businesses.

www.HBLTCI.com — Learn more about Margie Barrie and her long-term care sales training at Hagelman Barrie Sales Training and Solutions.

www.sellinginaskirt.com — Judy Hoberman's site with information about her consulting and training.

www.ltc-cltc.com — Learn more about Harley Gordon and the Certified in Long-Term Care (CLTC) program.

www.genworth.com — Use the Genworth Financial Cost of Care calculator to view cost of care in your state.

www.FeederWorkshopSuccess.com — Learn about feeder workshops from Annette Bau.

www.MillionDollarRelationshipMarketingSystem.com — Learn about the relationship, referral and follow up system from Annette Bau.

www.womenwealthandgiving.com — Learn more about women, wealth and giving from Margaret May Damen.

www.dancingelephants.net — Learn more about sales training from Laura Posey.

www.financialsocialmedia.com — Learn more about how financial professionals can use social media with Amy McIlwain.

www.advisorylink-dfw.com — Learn more about Women's Advisory Boards from Gerry Myers.

www.Alphamom.com — Alpha Mom is a consumer lifestyle brand, new media and research company and website for moms and moms-to-be.

www.VibrantNation.com — Vibrant Nation is the leading online community for women 50 plus.

ABOUT THE AUTHOR

HOLLY BUCHANAN is the head of Buchanan Marketing LLC, a consultancy which helps companies successfully market and sell to women. She's spent the last decade studying the differences between men and women and how those differences affect how men and women respond to advertising and make purchasing decisions. Her innovative discovery techniques and vast market knowledge have propelled her to the top of her field.

Holly Buchanan is a popular speaker and writer. She is the co-author (along with Michele Miller) of *The Soccer Mom Myth — Today's Female Consumer: Who She Really Is, Why She Really Buys* and writes a popular blog — Marketing to Women Online. She speaks to numerous business groups across the country from Hoboken to Hawaii. With her signature wit and entertaining style, she translates the differences between men and women into actionable sales and marketing strategies.

Holly has worked with hundreds of clients including brands like Genworth Financial, American General Life, Waterford, GE Healthcare, and HP. Her current focus is the financial field and helping financial companies and professionals do an outstanding job of attracting, selling to and retaining women clients.

And she likes sushi. She has been known to eat twice her body weight in one sitting.

For other interesting tidbits about Holly Buchanan, visit **www.SellingFinancialServicesToWomen.com**.